Hydroponic Gardening

DIY Guide to Master Hydroponics
Indoors Cultivation From Beginner to Expert
Inexpensive Fast and Easy Garden Without Soil

Thiago P.K. Land

Images from iStock

© **Copyright 2021 by Thiago P.K. Land.
All right reserved.**

The work contained herein has been produced with the intent to provide relevant knowledge and information on the topic on the topic described in the title for entertainment purposes only. While the author has gone to every extent to furnish up to date and true information, no claims can be made as to its accuracy or validity as the author has made no claims to be an expert on this topic. Notwithstanding, the reader is asked to do their own research and consult any subject matter experts they deem necessary to ensure the quality and accuracy of the material presented herein.

This statement is legally binding as deemed by the Committee of Publishers Association and the American Bar Association for the territory of the United States. Other jurisdictions may apply their own legal statutes. Any reproduction, transmission, or copying of this material contained in this work without the express written consent of the copyright holder shall be deemed as a copyright violation as per the current legislation in force on the date of publishing and subsequent time thereafter. All additional works derived from this material may be claimed by the holder of this copyright.

The data, depictions, events, descriptions, and all other information forthwith are considered to be true, fair, and accurate unless the work is expressly described as a work of fiction. Regardless of the nature of this work, the Publisher is exempt from any responsibility of actions taken by the reader in conjunction with this work. The Publisher acknowledges that the reader acts of their own accord and releases the author and Publisher of any responsibility for the observance of tips, advice, counsel, strategies and techniques that may be offered in this volume.

Table of Contents

Introduction
Chapter 1: Basics of Hydroponics
   What Is Hydroponic Gardening?
   History of Hydroponics
   Benefits of Growing Plants Hydroponically
      No Soil Pollution
      Less Usage of Water
      Faster Growth Rate of Plants
      Proper Nutriment of Plants
      Easy Control Over pH Level of Water
      No Need of Weeding
      No Need for Pesticides, Herbicides and Insecticides
      Saves a lot of Time
      Climate Control
      Better Use of Space
      No Barrier on Location
   Drawbacks of Hydroponics
      Expensive
      Constant Vigilance and Maintenance
      Easily Prone to Water-Borne diseases
Chapter 2: Choosing the Right Hydroponic System
   Wicking System
   Water Culture
   Ebb and Flow System
   Drip System
   NFT or The Nutrient Film Technique
   Aeroponics
Chapter 3: Everything You Need to Know About Mediums, Nutrients, and Lighting
   Choosing the Right Medium
      Vermiculite
      Oasis Cubes
      Hydroton Clay Pebbles
      Perlite
      Coco Coir
      Rockwool

All About Nutrients
- Carbon
- Nitrogen
- Phosphorus
- Potassium
- Sulfur
- Calcium
- Magnesium

Setting Up Appropriate Lighting
- Lighting Needs Differ From One Plant to Another
- What Should You Look For in a Grow Light?
- Types of Grow Lights

Chapter 4: A Step-by-Step Guide to Build Your Own Hydroponic Garden

Things You Will Need to Build Your Hydroponic Setup
- Grow Tray
- Reservoir
- Air Pump
- Air Stone
- Growing Medium
- Monitoring Equipment
- Fertilizer and Nutrient Solution
- Lighting
- Timer
- Water Pump

Factors to Keep in Mind Before Setting Up Your Hydroponic Garden
- Consider the Space You Have
- Consider the Type of Plants You Want to Grow
- Keep Your Budget in Mind
- Think About How Much Time You Can Invest

DIY Hydroponic Systems
- Simple Wick System
- Deep Water Culture Setup
- Ebb and Flow System

Chapter 5: What Are the Best Plants for a Hydroponic System?

What to Grow and What Not to Grow?

Vegetables
- Lettuce
- Tomatoes

    Radishes
    Kale
    Cucumbers
    Spinaches
    Beans
    Peppers
    Celery
  Fruits
    Strawberries
    Blueberries
    Grapes
    Cantaloupes
  Herbs
    Chives
    Basil
    Mint
    Sage

Chapter 6: Pest Prevention
  Commonly Seen Pests in Hydroponic Systems and Some General Information on Them
    Aphids
    Whiteflies
    Spider Mites
    Fungus Gnats
    Thrips
  Practices That Will Prevent a Pest Infestation
    Try Wearing Clean Clothes
    Make Sure to Clean Up the Runoff, Spills, etc. Properly
    Make Sure That Your Plants Are Completely Clean
  Identifying Pest Problems
    Deficiency of Iron in Your Plants
    Ash Mold
    Powdery Mildew
    Root Rot
    Downy Mildew
  Tips to Control an Existing Pest Infestation

Chapter 7: Hydroponic Troubleshooting
  System Leaks
    Reservoirs
    Hose Fittings

    Power Issues
    Part Size
  Rusty Spots on Leaves
  Leaves Turning Yellow
    Magnesium Deficiency
    Iron Deficiency
    Nitrogen Deficiency
  White Spots on Leaves
  Algae
    How Does Algae Develop in the System?
    What Are Some Preventive Measures That You Can Take?
    How to Eliminate Algae From the System?

Chapter 8: Common Mistakes Hydroponic Beginners Make
  Not Paying Attention to pH Levels
  Buying Incorrect or Cheap Lighting Products
  Underestimating the Cost of Building the System
  Choosing the Wrong Plants
  Using Wrong Fertilizer
  Lack of Proper Sanitation
  Not Having the Enthusiasm to Learn

Conclusion

Introduction

Congratulations on purchasing *Hydroponic Gardening*, and thank you for putting your trust in this text as you begin your journey.

Do you want to grow healthy plants in your own home despite the unfavorable climatic conditions? Well, don't worry because hydroponic gardening is at your rescue. And it's a very easy process if you follow the right steps. All you need is enough nutrients, light, and water. Not everyone lives in the right type of climate for the growth of plants, but that doesn't mean you won't be able to grow your own crops. Hydroponics gives you the opportunity to grow plants indoors in a very controlled environment so that you can mimic the ideal growing conditions of that plant.

In this book, I will introduce you to the concept of hydroponics right from the basics. You will learn how to start your own hydroponic garden in a step-by-step process. You will also learn the pros and cons of this type of gardening and how it is better than traditional gardening procedures. All you need to do is have the enthusiasm to learn and commit yourself to follow the steps as stated.

There are plenty of books on this subject on the market, thanks again for choosing this one! Every effort was made to ensure it is full of as much useful information as possible; please enjoy!

Hydroponic vegetables growing in greenhouse

Chapter 1
Basics of Hydroponics

I know most of you reading this book have a hobby of gardening or are passionate about growing greens. You have come to the right place. This chapter will walk you through all the necessary details about a gardening technique that requires no soil. Yes, you read that right - growing plants in the absence of soil.

Hydroponic gardening is a technique that has allowed humans to grow healthy plants sans the soil. This is a hassle-free technique that takes up almost no space, and thus you can adapt to this method for growing plants inside or outside of your house. With the help of water and plant nutrients, edible plants can be easily grown by even those who are not that great at parenting plants.

As cool as it sounds, several scientific facts are stating that it can easily be the most preferred gardening method in the future. So, read on to learn the basics of the faster and better method of gardening - hydroponic gardening.

Lettuce hydroponic

What Is Hydroponic Gardening?

The term 'hydroponic' is the combination of the words hydro and ponos, both of which are derived from the Greek vocabulary. Hydro means water, and ponos mean toil or labor. Thus, the word 'hydroponic' means that the work is done by water and hence completely justifies the purpose of the method.

Hydroponic Gardening

As the name suggests, hydroponic gardening refers to the technique or method of gardening where all the labor or work of growing the plant is done by water. This process of cultivation does not require the presence of soil. A water-based solution that has all the necessary nutrients for the plant is enough to grow the plant.

Plants grown using the traditional methodology use soil as a growing medium, where it is required to hold the plant upright in its place. The roots of such plants grow in length as they seek water and nutrients in the soil. Plants grown indoors in tubs need constant watering to grow.

Thus, the water and nutrients are necessary and important for the plant to grow and not the soil. The underlying principle of hydroponically growing plants is the same - as long as the plant is receiving all the required minerals and water, it will thrive and grow into a healthy and beautiful plant. In fact, as a hydroponically grown plant does not need to seek out water and minerals, it grows faster as it uses all the energy in growing the stem part rather than the root part.

Most plants or herbs that are grown hydroponically are usually grown in greenhouses or other similar controlled environments. This is because the plants need to be kept at a certain temperature, which varies for different plants.

There are a few other requirements that need to be satisfied to grow healthy plants hydroponically. The basic requirements are:

1. **Fresh Water** - We are talking about hydroponic gardening, so water has to be the first requirement. However, for this specific method of gardening, we need fresh or pure water that has an optimal pH. The pH level of the water may vary somewhere between 5.8 to 6.5, but the optimum is considered to be 6.3. Water with the proper power of hydrogen (pH) is required as it helps the verdure to absorb nutrients properly.

   An imbalance in the pH of the water may cause some of the nutrients to not reach the plant properly, leading to deficiency of those minerals in the sapling. This will therefore reflect in the growth and health of the plant. It is therefore extremely important to keep a proper check on the pH level of the water. This might seem a task, but even soils need to have a certain pH value to allow certain plants to grow on them.

   It is easier to keep a check on the pH level of water than soil. There are numerous pH measuring meters that are easily in the local stores or even in the hydroponic stores and the hardware stores. Check the potential of hydrogen in the water.

If it is higher than 6.5 or 6.8, then it implies the water is more basic than the allowed basicity. It can be easily fixed by adding acids like phosphoric acid to the water. If the pH level is lower than 5.8, then the water has turned more acidic. In that case, fix the water's pH by adding base like an iota of dissolvable potash.

I have named the acids and bases that I think are easily available in the market, but you may go ahead with another option as well. Just remember that to lower the pH, you will need to add some acidic soluble to the water, and higher the pH level of water, you need to add a base to the liquid. Keep checking the pH level of the water frequently or at least in a week.

2. **Oxygen** - Oxygen is required for photosynthesis (the process of making their food by plants). Roots of traditionally grown plants get the required oxygen from it as there are many pores in the soil. But that is not the case with water. So, to maintain a proper supply of oxygen to the plants, you may invest in an air pump or an air stone.

These supplies are easily available in the market as many hydroponic supply stores sell types of equipment required to oxygenate hydroponic plants. However, this may be avoided by leaving some breathable space between the roots and the water or the solution. The simplest way of ensuring that the plants are getting enough oxygen is to not completely drown the roots of the plants in the solution.

3. **Root Support or Growing Medium** - Owing to the increasing popularity of the gardening technique, several hydroponic systems have been developed. Depending on the system, you may or may not need root support. Growing medium, however, is a must that can allow the plant to stand tall and upright while also allowing aeration.

    Depending on the system, you may easily skip root support and indirectly bring the root in contact with the water solution. The plant needs to be held upright with the help of tubs or suspenders. The other types of hydroponic systems require some form of substitution of soil. There are many options to choose from, like Rockwool, vermiculite, coconut fiber (often referred to as coir), clay pebbles, perlite, and peat moss. Other than Rockwool, all the other options are affordable. Some gardeners even prefer types of sands as a support to the roots of the plants. I will discourage using it until you have no other choice, as it gets dense.

4. **Sunlight or Artificial Lights** - Just like temperature, some hydroponically growing plants need a specific amount of light exposure. This will not be a problem if you are making your

soil-less garden outside the house, but if the garden is inside the house premises, then you need to pay some attention to it. You may also have to invest in some artificial lighting. The DLI or Daily Light Integral refers to the process of fixing up the artificial lights depending on the required light placements.

5. **Nutrients** - Nutrients like phosphorus, magnesium, calcium, etc., are required for the plant's growth. In traditional farming or gardening, we usually add fertilizers and pesticides to the soils. Fertilizers are plant food. Similarly, plant supplements are also needed by saplings growing in this process.

The advantage of growing plants in this process is that you gradually learn to recognize your plants' needs. According to their needs, the gardener may easily mix the necessary supplements with water to make their nutrient-rich solution.

Other than that, there is another option of buying ready-made nutrient solvents. This is a bit more convenient as all the nutrients are packed in a single unit, and all that has to be done is to mix them in the water.

Other than these basic requirements, depending on the setup of the gardening system, you may encounter a few other things like containers, grow lights, or a reservoir. Some of the common hydroponic gardening systems are:

1. The EBB and Flow System (active system)

2. The Wick system (passive system)

3. Continuous Drip System of Hydroponic gardening (active non-recovery or recovery system)

4. Nutrient Film Technique (another active type system)

Here, the active system refers to the system that moves along the nutrients and usually involves small pumps or generators. The passive system does not have this component and mostly delivers nutrients to the plants through wicks or tubes like structures. The passive system of soil-less gardening holds back more liquid than the active systems and thus is less efficient than the latter system.

History of Hydroponics

We are practicing modern hydroponics gardening but do you know that this method of gardening has been in existence for thousands of years? Several instances go on to prove that this is not a recent finding but has continued to exist since 600 BC.

Hydroponic Gardening

Babylon's infamous Hanging garden is perhaps the earliest example of soilless gardening. There are several other instances of this method of farming around 1100 AD. The term that we use today to describe soil-less farming was coined somewhere during the 1920 and 1930.

The term was coined by Mr. William F. Gericke of U.C. Berkley. Around the mid-nineties, this method was well known enough to be used to grow crops. These crops were grown to be supplied to the troops stuck in the Wake Islands, in the Pacific Ocean.

The popularity and scope of development of this method of crop cultivation started to pick up pace after that. Since then, many scientists have performed several kinds of research on this methodology and found out various systems. Modern formulas of providing nutrients to plants have also been recorded. The latest update came from NASA, who declared that the hydroponic technique is the best suitable technique for growing crops and providing them to spacemen on mars.

Benefits of Growing Plants Hydroponically

Some of you might be wondering that soilless gardening is cool, but why should we shift to it, right? Well, the number of proven advantages that hydroponic gardening has is profuse. When compared to traditional soil-based gardening, soilless gardening has more advantages over the prior. Some of the definite advantages of growing plants hydroponically are:

No Soil Pollution

Farming causes serious soil erosion. Constant planting of different crops on the same piece of soil deprives the soil of all its nutrients and makes it unfit for cultivation. The hydroponic farming technique is soil-less; thus, clearly, there is no involvement or requirement of topsoil. Thus, no soil or topsoil erosion as well.

When soil becomes unfit for cultivation due to excess planting, this will be the only process of cultivation that humans will be left with. I have referred to this method of cultivation as the future cultivation method numerous times in the article, wondered why? Because NASA is considering this soil-less technique as the way of growing crops in space or outside earth.

Less Usage of Water

If you google the details of water usage, then you will learn that about 80% of water usage in the United States is done in traditional soil farming. If the US started hydroponic farming, then this figure will be reduced by 10%. This could be a big step towards saving drinkable water on the planet.

Water sprinkled on the ground is mostly lost due to evaporation, water rolling, and many other reasons. That is not the case with this farming technique as in it, the roots of the plant are brought in direct contact with water. Also, as plants do not need to seek water through the soil, it grows healthier than it would have on the soil.

Faster Growth Rate of Plants

Due to several factors like the optimum temperature, great oxygen supply, zero pests, weeds, or insects, and optimum amount of nutrients reaching all ends of the plant, hydroponic plants grow at a 30% increased rate than plants grown on soil. Examples of few plants that grow almost 50% faster when cultivated by soil-less techniques are tomato and lettuce.

Proper Nutriment of Plants

Vegetation grown through this process receives optimum nutrients as nutrients are dissolved in the water that the plant roots are in direct contact with. This also causes the plants to have an improved yield.

Easy Control Over pH Level of Water

The pH of water can be easily measured using pH meters and adjusted accordingly by mixing the right substances. This ensures that all the nutrients dissolved in the water are getting absorbed by the plants.

No Need of Weeding

Seeds of weeds need soil and all other substances like plants to germinate and grow. Hydroponic gardening is soil-less, where the germinated seedlings of plants are brought in contact with the nutrient-rich solution for them to grow.

Without soil and the germination of the seeds, weeds have no scope to grow. Thus, in this process of gardening, there is no weed growth alongside the plants. Thus, all the nutrients are preserved and received by the plants alone.

No Need for Pesticides, Herbicides, and Insecticides

Hydroponic plants are mostly grown indoors in greenhouses that have controlled environments. This eradicates any chances of insect attack and protects the young bud or trees from birds and pests like groundhogs and gophers. With these problems at bay, there is no need for pesticides, insecticides, or herbicides. The fruits and vegetables that we are growing are completely healthy as they are free from chemicals.

Saves a lot of Time

This method saves a lot of time and energy that a gardener would have otherwise had to invest if they had to barber weeds. The task of weed removal overtiring as trimming, plowing, tilling, and hoeing takes a long time. It also saves us from the trouble of spreading pesticides and insecticides.

Climate Control

As I have already mentioned before, vegetation grown through this technique enjoys a controlled environment tailored to their specific needs. The nutrients, the light, and even oxygen levels that the plant is exposed to are controlled. This ensures that crops can be grown all season long and in greater numbers as optimum climates speed up their growth. Perfect climatic conditions also help in the production of perfectly healthy plants that are free from any kind of soil-borne diseases.

Better Use of Space

Crop cultivation on the ground requires the plant to grow at certain distances to let each plant get nutrients from the soil. Thus, even though the area is huge due to limitations, the density is less. This is not a problem for clay-less farming, where the density of crop grown can be adjusted according to the will of the farmer. Thus, it is also safe to say that this farming technique does not take up much space; instead, it helps to maximize the available farming space by allowing the increased density of planting.

No Barrier on Location

Owing to the nutrient and water solution and the controlled environment, a gardener need not worry about the soil or weather conditions that would be suitable for the growth of the plant.

Drawbacks of Hydroponics

Like every other method, hydroponic gardening also has a few handful demerits that are almost insignificant compared to the number of advantages of the method. Some of the prominent disadvantages of this method are:

Expensive

The cost of setting up the hydroponic system can be expensive. It involves a lot of components like the growing medium, containers, pumps, artificial lights, and air refineries. If you intend to start a business, you might also need to buy a digital pH level checker, which can cost about ninety to a hundred dollars.

However, the good thing is that some of these are just one-time investments, whereas some are optional. If you want to have self-grown healthy fruits and vegetables that are free from any chemicals, then these expenses are profitable for your health in the long run.

Constant Vigilance and Maintenance

Constant vigilance is required as you have to measure the pH level of the water and micro-monitor the minutest of changes in the temperature and the lights. Soil-grown plants are better in this respect as they do not need this constant attention. The soil protects the roots from high temperatures and any other environmental changes.

In the case of clay-less farming, these things have to be monitored remotely by the gardener. Else the health of the plant will be hampered. In this method, the roots of the plants have no other source of obtaining nutrition other than the nutrition provided to them by mixing it with the water. The deficiency of any nutrient reflects on the plant quickly and easily. Thus, the maintenance of these plants is much higher than that of soil-grown plants.

Easily Prone to Water-Borne diseases

Hydroponically grown plants are completely free from soil-borne diseases, but they are not free from water-borne diseases. The primary substance that is supporting their growth and health is the water. If the water is somehow infected, then the infection will spread in the plant stem easily and quickly (within hours).

Since all the plants are grown within the same system that is connected through the water channel, infections spread rapidly through the water. It takes just a few hours for all the plants to get infected by the same water-borne disease. If the condition worsens, all the plants might die within hours from the spread of the infection or disease.

So, if you have failed at growing your favorite vegetable or fruit plants numerous times, using the traditional method, try planting it again using the hydroponic gardening style. It requires less space and hence is an excellent option for those who want to have interior gardening. It also requires fewer efforts as you need not uproot the wild plants or weeds at regular intervals.

Owing to the factor that it requires no soil and can allow the cultivation of crops throughout the season, it is soon going to be the favorite option among most farmers, making it the most suitable option for future farming. Many farmers and giants have already started producing crops using this technique of hydroponic gardening. It is possible that you have already tasted fruits or vegetables that are grown hydroponically.

Wandering how come you noticed no difference in these eatables from traditionally grown fruits and vegetables? Because there is no difference as such, both are organically grown and taste the same. So, if you are still wondering whether or not to opt for this soil-less method of gardening, the answer is you should. You must try out this gardening and contribute towards the well-being of the environment by not contributing to topsoil erosion.

Thiago P.K. Land

Chapter 2
Choosing the Right Hydroponic System

Now that we have covered the basics of hydroponics in the previous chapter, here we will talk about the different types of hydroponic systems there in the world. We will see the advantages and disadvantages of all of them so that you can decide which one of them is right for you. No matter what your choice, you need to keep in mind that it should be at par with your experience, needs, and budget.

There are a total of six different types of hydroponic systems, and we are going to talk about each of them in-depth.

Sticky note on concrete wall, Advantages Disadvantages

Wicking System

Let's start with the most basic and easy form of hydroponic systems first – the wicking system. This one is perfect for beginners. If you don't want to worry about complex processes and yet want a taste of hydroponics, then this system is just what you need.

This type of hydroponic system does not have any moving part in it and is thus referred to as a passive hydroponic system. This factor itself makes wicking systems much more user-friendly since you do not have to do much to maintain them, and they are comparatively cheaper to build as well. The best thing

Hydroponic Gardening

about this system is that you can build it simply out of some common household components, and it comprises only four parts that we are going to see here.

The four main parts or components that make up a wick hydroponic system are as follows –

- Reservoir to store the nutrient solution
- Growing container
- Wicks
- Growing medium

Now let us have a look at how this system works. The main working principle that is followed here is capillary action. That is how the nutrient solution from the reservoir is taken up and reaches the roots of the plants in this system. Capillary action is a very simple mechanism, and all of us have experienced it unknowingly. Every time paper towels or sponges absorb water, remember that it is happening because of capillary action. The same mechanism is also used in candles where the wick draws wax from the main body, and this is also how the name has been derived.

So, you can build this system very easily. First, take a growing tray and then choose a substrate. It can be anything like coco coir, vermiculite, or perlite, and then fill the growing tray with it. All of these mediums work really well for this hydroponic setup because they do not remain extremely soggy, and their wicking capacity is excellent. After that, take a container filled with water and keep it below the growing medium. Your plants will take the water from this container. The water tray and the grow tray need to be connected, and for this connection, you will have to use wicks. You can take nylon or cotton wicks for this purpose as both of them serve really well. The number of wicks in the system will have to be proportionately increased depending on the number of plants you have.

Some of the various advantages of this hydroponic system are –

- The system is lucid.

- By using a porous growing medium, the rate of absorption of oxygen by the plants can be ameliorated.

- Budget-friendly as you may not need to bear the extra cost of setting up lights or electricity bills if the system set up is at a place where it receives ample natural light.

- The area is not a problem as the wick system can be set up in small areas as well. In fact, by simply recycling a few items, you can make a fully functional wick system all by yourself for your home.

- Suitable for beginners as it does not require much maintenance and is easy to understand.

Some of the disadvantages of this system are –

- The system is easy to build and maintain, but the yields obtained from it are comparatively lesser than that of what is yielded by other hydroponic systems.

- Not all plants respond well to the roots remaining moist at all times. Such plants do not grow well in the wick system, the roots, and thus the plant starts to decay.

- Growing big plants with the help of this system is tough, and you may have to increase the level of oxygenation to let the plants grow.

- Constant surveillance is required to maintain the optimum nutrients in the reservoir.

- The wick system may become susceptible to mold growth, fungal infestations, and even rot if the water fails to circulate properly.

Water Culture

The water culture is yet another hydroponic system, which due to the ease of set up and simple concept, is preferred by small-scale gardeners as well as by commercial cultivators. The unique property of this system is that although the system's concept is simple, it can be scaled up by building the system with a variety of materials.

The concept is simple as all that is required to be done is suspend the plants right above the reservoir. The factor that contributes to the success of this system is that the roots sit in the nutrient solution throughout the day. This ensures that the plant is receiving all the necessary nutrients and oxygen in plenty.

The main parts or components that make up a water culture hydroponic system are as follows –

- Reservoir to store nutrient solution with a covering lid having holes (or Styrofoam)
- Air stones or an aquarium air pump (for aeration) or falling water (typically used by commercial growers for aeration)
- Air hose
- Growing container (cups, baskets, or pots)
- Growing medium

The working of the system is extremely easy to understand and can be easily enhanced through creative thinking. The reservoir holds the water, rich in nutrients, which is necessary and important for the plant to thrive. Even though there could be many options to choose from to suspend the plants, the most common suspension material used by water culture using growers is Styrofoam. The styrofoams are floated on top of the reservoir, and the roots are dangling through into the solution. The roots of the plants grown through this system have to be submerged in the nutrient solution throughout the twenty-four hours of the day and through the week.

Thus, the other possible way of achieving this is by covering the container of the nutrient solution with a lid that has slits in it. The plant is resting on a basket right on top of the lid, and the roots are submerged into the nutritive solution through these slits or holes. The roots do not decay from the continuous submission in the liquid due to the air bubbles that arise in the solution. These roots are also saved from suffocation as the nutrient solution also contains dissolved oxygen.

The key working principle of this system is - the greater the number of air bubbles in the nutritive water-based solution, the better it is for the health of the plant. Therefore, the grower needs to ensure that there is a constant rising of air bubbles in the solution.

This can be achieved easily through the help of an aquarium air pump. Another factor affecting the plant's growth is the size of the bubbles - the smaller they are, the better they will be for the plants. The reason being the minute bubbles are easier to get absorbed by the roots of the plants.

Try to maintain a continuous flow of air bubbles in the solution, which are as compact as possible, and for further better functioning of the system, try to ensure the air bubbles are reaching the roots. This means that the bubbles should come in direct contact with the plant root.

Before moving on to the pros and cons of the system, another thing that needs mention under this hydroponic system is the DWC, which is the abbreviation for Deep Water Culture. It is simply one of the most common variations of the water culture hydroponic system. This variation is popular amongst and practiced mostly by hydroponic gardening hobbyists and is helpful for growing big plants.

As the name already mentions (deep water), this variation consists of a basket that is capable of holding more gallons of water. The difference between a normal water culture system and this variation of the system is that the latter is usually having a water drop of 8 to 10 inches. The most popular bucket used to build this system being the one that can hold five gallons of water.

Hydroponic Gardening

Another reason for the variation having the name is the fact that the roots of the plants grown via this system are completely submerged in the water (that is, submerged deep in the water). Usually, big plants have roots that are scattered more; this deep level of water, therefore, provides more space for the roots to boom and continue to grow.

Some of the various advantages of this hydroponic system are:

- The structure of the system is simple and has no nozzles or feeder lines. This is a big advantage for the system as this allows the system to remain free from any sort of clogging.

- There are no clogging or complicated pieces of equipment involved in the system, making it easy to maintain. Thus, once the system is set up nicely, not much effort is needed to maintain it.

- The roots remain submerged in water 24*7 hours, ensuring the plant is well hydrated and nourished. Therefore, not much fertilizer is required.

- As we observed above, the system doesn't contain that many movable parts. Hence, the assembly is less.

- The dissolved oxygen in the water and the continuous upward movement of the air bubbles build a good aeration administration in the system thereby, enhancing the absorption rate of the plants' roots and improving the rate of cell growth.

- Due to the direct and continuous supply of all the necessary nutrients to the plants, they grow faster than they would have if they were grown by the traditional soil gardening technique. Say you sow lettuce on the soil. How long do you think it will take before the arrival of the harvesting time? Almost after two months (60 days), right? But if you grow the plant through this system, the harvesting period will arrive in half the number of days. It means the plant will be fully grown within a month. So, the harvesting speed is almost doubled when plants are grown by this model.

Some of the disadvantages of the water culture system are:

- The major factor contributing to the growth of the plants is the air bubbles generated by the air pumps. Thus, the air pump is an integral part of the system. If it collapses, the entire system and the plants will collapse in a matter of hours. Thus, it should be ensured that the air pump has been replaced as quickly as possible if it stops working.

- Another major disadvantage is that the water-based nutrition solution can easily get warmer than the optimum temperature. This is due to the presence of the submersible pump in the water for a continuous prolonged time. Maintaining the temperature at an optimum can be challenging to obtain and can only be achieved only when the system is circulating properly.

- Continuous surveillance may be required for the smaller-scale water culture hydroponic system to maintain the water level, the pH level of the water, and even the concentration of the nutrients in the solvent.

- Another major problem of the smaller-scale versions of the system is the high chances of over-calibration and under-calibration trouble.

Ebb and Flow System

Also known as the flood and drain system, the Ebb and flow hydroponic system works exactly as the name suggests. The entire system pendulums between a span of flooding cycle and a periodic draining. It is the most popular hydroponic gardening system among all the cultivators - the hobbyists and the beginners. There are pretty good reasons for the system's immense popularity among the masses, the prime reason being the fact that it can be built from scratch by using the matters present with you. Not just that, the entire process of assembling the system is also relatively easy.

The main parts or components that make up an ebb and flow hydroponic system are as follows –

- Growing container
- Reservoir to store the nutrient solution
- Pond or fountain that can be used to submerge containers
- A timer operated pump
- Growing medium
- A tube-like structure to help flood the reservoir
- Another tube for helping in setting the water level

To build the flood and drain system, start by taking any available material or container. These shall be used as our grow beds. Fill it with the preferred growing medium. Now comes the flooding tube. With its help, the grow bed is supplied (or flooded) with a water-based nutrient solution. The tube fills water in the grow bed when the timer-operated pump is activated and continues to fill the bed for the predetermined time set in the timer.

To avoid the overflow of the nutrient solution, the small hole towards the top of the bed drains the solution with the help of a tube. When the flooding tube stops, the solution is completely drained out of

Hydroponic Gardening

the system. The entire cycle is repeated at intervals determined by the timer.

Some of the various advantages of this hydroponic system are:

- The cost of building the system is almost negligible as with the proper plan; it can be built just by the materials already available to you.

- Not much technical knowledge needs to be acquired to understand and maintain the system.

- Plants that are constantly thirsty for water will thrive well in this system of hydroponic gardening.

- The entire system can be easily modified at any point in time and can even be upgraded at a minimum cost when compared to the upgradation cost of other hydroponic systems.

Some of the disadvantages of the Ebb and flow system are:

- Since the water level is dynamic, it can get very difficult to manage the optimum pH level of the water.

- The timer-based pump plays a major role in the system. The collapse of this pump can hamper the entire system.

- The continued flooding and draining of the nutrition-rich solution causes some of the nutrition to get left behind in the growing bed. These accumulate and form clogs that prevent the roots from being able to absorb the nutrients properly from the fresh flood of water.

Drip System

The drip system for soilless gardening is the same as for cultivation on soil. The immense popularity of the system is due to the ease at which it can be scaled up or down. Even though it can be used for both homegrown and commercially grown hydroponic plants, it is mostly used by commercial cultivators.

The main parts or components that make up the drip system are as follows –

- Growing containers for each plant

- Reservoir to store the nutrient solution

- A submersible pump (will be timer operated)

- Flexible or PVC tubing

- Growing medium

The construction of this system is fairly simple - sow the plants in individual containers. Each pot has a dedicated drip emitter which is regulated by the timer-operated pump.

Some of the various advantages of this system are:

- The amount of manual work and maintenance is lower than all other hydroponic systems as everything is automated.

- It can be easily scaled up or down depending on the requirement.

- The chances of its failure are lower than all other hydroponic systems mentioned here.

- Requires minimum usage of water even while plants are grown.

Some of the disadvantages of the drip system are:

- Not very suitable for small-scale or home-based hydroponic gardens.

NFT or The Nutrient Film Technique

NFT has channels holding the plants in a tilted manner while the rhizomes (roots) of the plants are hanging. Water and nutrients are made to flow through the channel where the roots are allowed to pick up or absorb any amount of nutrient that they require. Now the concern may arise whether this system can provide the proper amount of nutrients to the plants. The answer is yes! The root remains moist throughout as the tilted channel through which the liquid flows are maintained with high humidity.

Some of the various advantages of this hydroponic system are:

- Supervision becomes easier since the roots are hanging and are visible to the naked eye.

- The system does not require or waste much water and nutrients.

- With this system, the process of purifying and sterilizing the system is simple.

- The pH of the water remains maintained organically.

- The instances of clogging in this system are very low.

Some of the disadvantages of the NFT or the nutrient film system are –

- If due to some reason, there is water cut in the system, the plants will start drooping rapidly.

- Not suitable for plants whose roots tend to boom suddenly. This is so as the rapidly growing roots are likely to choke the channels.

Aeroponics

The concept of an aeroponics system is very simple but requires some prior technical knowledge to be able to build it. This system requires no growing medium as the plants are suspended in the air through the collar effect. The tricky part is that the plant needs to be provided with the right amount of nutrition by spraying water. As there is no continuous water supply, the spraying of water and nutrients has to be carried out at regular intervals.

Some of the various advantages of aeroponics hydroponic system are:

- It can be used in congested areas as it helps to use the available space to its maximum potential.

- The plants grow rapidly in this system, and therefore there is a much higher yield. This is due to the continuous supply of oxygen to the roots and the plant.

- The process of cleaning the system is hassle-free.

- Unlike all the other systems of hydroponic, aeroponics does not require a growing medium.

Sans the growing medium, the pace of nutrient absorption by the roots is increased.

Some of the disadvantages of the aeroponics system are:

- The chamber where the rhizomes reside needs to be disinfected at regular intervals.

- The system gravely suffers from frequent power outages.

- The initial cost of setting the aeroponics system up is very high.

- Constant surveillance is required to ensure the pH levels and also the nutrient level.

- Not suitable for beginners or people with no prior technical knowledge.

Chapter 3
Everything You Need to Know About Mediums, Nutrients, and Lighting

Before you build your own hydroponic system, there are three of the most important things that you need to familiarize yourself with – mediums, nutrients, and lighting. We will cover all three aspects in this chapter.

Choosing the Right Medium

A hydroponic system doesn't involve the use of soil, as you already know. Here, you need to substitute the soil with something known as the growing medium so that the roots of your plants can be embedded in them. The most important advantage of not having to use soil is that there is no need for you to worry about soilborne disease-causing microorganisms or any bacteria. While choosing the right medium, you need to check for these characteristics – aeration properties, cation exchange capacity, moisture absorption rates, drainage capabilities, etc. Here are some good medium options for you to consider if you are planning to build a hydroponic system.

Vermiculite

Vermiculite has a high cation exchange capacity. As a result, several minerals get reserved in this medium and released later when the plant needs them. Vermiculite closely resembles mica because of its layered appearance.

Advantages of Using Vermiculite as a Medium of Your Hydroponic System

- Vermiculite has an amazing water retention capacity that makes it a perfect medium for a lot of hydroponic systems. It is a sterile medium and has a neutral pH range.

- It has a unique nutrient retention capacity. It is also known for paving the way for enhancing root growth.

- It is responsible for offering good root anchorage and preventing the development of molds and mildew.

- This medium has good versatility as well.

Disadvantages of Using Vermiculite as a Medium of Your Hydroponic System

- It is a little costly.

- Vermiculite is not a renewable source as it originates from the ores. So, a time will come when this product might not be available anymore.

- Working with vermiculite involves several health hazards as well.

- Sometimes, because of too much moisture retention, the plants might get damaged.

Oasis Cubes

multi-coloured foam cloning collars for hydroponics and aeroponics

Waterlogging doesn't happen fast in this medium. These can be used as starter cubes for your hydroponic system. They can even be used for the entire system if the conditions are supportive. Oasis cubes are similar to the foam used in holding the flowers in flower displays. Oasis cubs can wick moisture and can also absorb both air and water quickly. Oasis cubes can be used for the propagation of the seeds in the case of commercial hydroponic gardens. Oasis cubes are usually used for crops that take a short time to germinate, like lettuce.

Hydroponic Gardening

Advantages of Using Oasis Cubes as a Medium of Your Hydroponic System

- Oasis cubes are going to be an excellent choice in case you are searching for a medium for starting with the seeds or for propagating the cuttings.

- The process of germination gets accelerated because of the oasis cubes.

- Oasis cubes don't need to be soaked before you use them.

- Oasis cubes have a neutral pH range.

- These cubes have amazing water retention capacity that is approximately 30 to 40 times the original weight of these cubes.

- This medium enhances the root development in the early stages of the life of a plant.

Disadvantages of Using Oasis Cubes as a Medium of Your Hydroponic System

- Oasis cubes are not environment-friendly. They are somewhat similar to Styrofoam in this respect.

- Reusing them is possible, but it demands an unreasonable cost.

Hydroton Clay Pebbles

Pile of Expanded Clay Aggregate

Hydroton clay pebbles are of the same size as marbles or peanuts. They are one of the best mediums for transplanting or harvesting because of their lightweight nature.

Advantages of Using Hydroton Clay Pebbles as a Medium of Your Hydroponic System

- Their pore spaces are large, thereby ensuring no blockage of any kind. If you are building the Ebb and Flow system, Hydroton is the best option for you.

- This medium has a good air-holding capacity, due to which the root zones are always well-oxygenated. It also offers great percolation, which lessens the chances of forming the anaerobic zones.

- Hydroton clay pebbles are actually made from clay, which is widely abundant and is renewable. Therefore, it is an environment-friendly medium. So, even if you are using these pebbles on a large scale, it doesn't matter to the earth.

- This medium is also reusable. But before reusing them, you need to rinse these pebbles in order to remove any build-ups.

- If you use this medium for harvesting, pulling your plants out will not at all be troublesome. This is because it is a loose medium.

Disadvantages of Using Hydroton Clay Pebbles as a Medium of Your Hydroponic System

- Hydroton clay pebbles don't have a good water retention capacity. As a result, your plants might dry or wilt if you don't water them regularly. If the plant you are planning to grow has a high transpiration rate or is a water-hungry plant, this is not the right choice of medium for you.

- Working with this medium might be easy, but it is very costly compared to the other mediums. As a result, small growers might not be able to afford it.

- After installation, it might float for the first 1 or 2 months. At any point of time, these pebbles might get sucked into the drainage lines. This might lead to blockage problems in the drains.

Perlite

perlite for hydroponics

It is a volcanic glass that, when heated, expands like popcorn. Perlite is quite affordable compared to the other mediums of hydroponic systems. Perlite is usually used after mixing them with some other medium. Since it is an affordable option, people choose it while building a wick hydroponic system, requiring less investment.

Advantages of Using Perlite as a Medium of Your Hydroponic System

- Perlite is reusable. The only situation when you can't reuse it anymore is when it gets affected by some pest or develops some disease problem.

- When you are using perlite, it is going to help you to deal with anaerobic conditions. Perlite has a coarse texture and has an amazing air-holding capacity. No matter your plant is growing in water or soil, anaerobic conditions arise when there is a shortage of oxygen. If you want to keep your plants alive, it is important to eliminate the anaerobic zones.

- Perlite is very cheap (the price of perlite is almost half of the price of Hydroton for the same amount). The requirement of perlite is less too. So, it is an affordable and cost-effective medium option.

- You don't obtain perlite from some sort of organic source, thereby eliminating the chances of your plant getting fungal or pest infections.

- This medium has a neutral pH range.

Disadvantages of Using Perlite as a Medium of Your Hydroponic System

- Perlite is non-renewable since it is an ore. Eventually, a time will come when there will be no availability of perlite.

- Perlite is composed of small-sized particles. So, the pore spaces might get blocked if your plant has an aggressive root system. Not just the root system, but it can even lead to blocked percolation because of the accumulation of things like biofilm, algae, and debris.

- You have to always wear a mask while working with perlite because it can cause certain health hazards when inhaled.

Coco Coir

Coconut Coir Husk

Now, we are going to talk about a medium known as coco coir, which is used by a lot of hydroponic systems because of various good reasons. Before jumping to the reasons, let me tell you what it is actually. Basically, coco coir is a byproduct of coconut fiber. At first, the coconut fiber is torn out from the coconut shells. Coco coir is then manufactured. After the extraction of the coir from the coconut shell, the growing substrate is pulverized. At first, the coconut is retted, and then the husk pulp decomposes through the natural curing process. Then the fibers are removed from the coconut shells using steel combs. After collecting the fibers, they are dried. Then they are either pressed for casting them into different shapes or are sold as loose mulch.

Here are the various types of coco coir that you can use in your hydroponic system.

1. **Coco Peat** – It has a brown color, and its appearance is similar to peat moss. It is a dense product and hence has an excellent water retention capacity.

2. **Coco Fibers** – Coco fibers are sold as stringy coconut fiber bundles. The main characteristic of coco fibers is that oxygen can easily penetrate the plant roots with the help of these coco fibers. With time, these fibers will eventually break down because fibers are usually not very absorbent.

3. **Coco Chips** – These are shaped like small coir chunks. They have all the good qualities of both fibers and peat. The water retention capacity is excellent, and it has a lot of space for air pockets as well.

You can use a mixture of them as well for increasing the benefits.

Advantages of Using Coco Coir as a Medium of Your Hydroponic System

- If you are planning to use coco coir for drain-to-waste growing, you will get excellent results.

- It is a very popular medium for hydroponic systems because of the combinations of its properties. In addition to ensuring good drainage, it also ensures adequate aeration. The water retention capacity is good as well. As a result, the plant roots get enough exposure to the air and get plenty of room to grow.

- Coco coir has a neutral pH range (5.2 to 6.8).

- It is made from the part of the coconut that usually goes wasted, thereby making it an environmentally conscious product. A tree produces almost 150 coconuts in one year.

- Coco coir can even be reused if appropriately treated.

- Coco coir has antifungal properties that prevent the roots of the plant from getting attacked by pests.

Disadvantages of Using Coco Coir as a Medium of Your Hydroponic System

- Make sure to do your research about the production process or coco coir before you start using it as a medium for your hydroponic system.

If the husks were immersed in saltwater, it might affect the plants. You have to make sure that the coco coir was washed thoroughly in fresh water.

- Coco coir has a high cation exchange rate. As a result, it might hold some nutrients like iron, calcium, and magnesium. So, while using this medium, make sure that your plant isn't getting deficient in these nutrients and is getting them in adequate amounts.

- Coco coir sometimes undergoes chemical treatment before they are sold. If that is the case, it might harm your plant.

Rockwool

Sheet of Rockwool

It is the most popular medium used in hydroponic systems. The main component of this medium is basalt. Rockwool also comprises chalk and salt. Basalt is a fine-grained rock formed from volcanic activities. For making Rockwool, the basalt rock is spun into thin threads, resembling cotton candies. Rockwool was introduced for the first time in the 1960s by the fiberglass industry. Initially, it was used for home insulation as an insulator material. The most important thing that makes it a suitable medium for a hydroponic system is that it never gets saturated.

Advantages of Using Rockwool as a Medium of Your Hydroponic System

- Rockwool has a high water-retaining capacity and also has the capacity to hold air. If you witness an equipment failure situation, the water-retaining capacity of Rockwool will be a savior in such a situation. If the Rockwool is partially submerged, it can hold up to 18% to 25% of air. So, there will always be enough oxygen.

- A wide range of size options is available for this medium for you to choose from. You can go for small cubes or even large slabs, depending on your hydroponic system.

Disadvantages of Using Rockwool as a Medium of Your Hydroponic System

- Rockwool is actually a rock, and so it isn't biodegradable. So, the disposal is problematic.

- Rockwool has a high pH value that you need to always keep in mind while you prepare the nutrient solution. You need to keep monitoring the pH continuously because the pH of this medium can change frequently. You need to always wear a mask while working with this medium because it has a lot of health hazards.

All About Nutrients

In a hydroponic system, for best results, specific nutrients are required that accelerate the growth of plants and render them a good and happy life. One of the most important things that need to be kept in mind in this system is the correct ratio of nutrients given to plants. The nutrient needed by the plants doesn't remain the same throughout the plant's life cycle, the proportions and types of nutrients change at different phases of germination like the nutrients that are essential during vegetative state varies from those of the flowering stage. It is suggested to have a clear idea about all the concepts if you are growing plants hydroponically. The main concern behind the usage of the right quantity and right kind of nutrients is that the plants are growing without soil, failing to receive the nutrients present in the soil already. As a result, the plants depend completely on you for their energy and nutrients. Nevertheless, the plants get affected even if correct nutrients are given at a specific time because plants may not absorb the nutrients due to certain issues relating to nutrient uptake that has recently been dealt with by the root zone environment.

All plants need few indispensable nutrients that scientists have categorized into three major parts in accordance to the relative amount of the nutrients needed by plants –

1. Macronutrients or the primary nutrients are the most significant nutrients required in larger amounts. They are carbon, nitrogen, potassium, oxygen, and phosphorus.

2. Secondary nutrients are required in moderate amounts. They are calcium, magnesium, and sulfur.

3. Micronutrients are also known as trace elements. They are required in small proportions than others but are fundamental for development and growth. They are boron, chlorine, copper, iron, manganese, molybdenum, zinc, nickel, sodium, silicon, cobalt.

Lesser or more nutrients will hamper the evolution of plants. For instance, too much nitrogen can increase the growth of leaves and simultaneously lead to reduced or no final products. Excess of manganese can turn the fruits and vegetables yellow causing gradual death. You need to be highly vigilant about the condition of plants and learn the immediate steps when in time of difficulty. A balanced diet for plants is crucial, and significant amendments in varying degrees are needed to be offered to the plants for standard output. You need to have proper knowledge about all nutrients, their traits, pros, and cons and apply in the time of need. You must know the difference between mobile and immobile nutrients, as they can greatly impact the plant. Some of the immobile elements are manganese, cobalt, sulfur, calcium, boron, chlorine. Some of the mobile elements are zinc, magnesium, phosphorus, potassium, nitrogen.

Here is some information about essential nutrients without which growth, development, production, and survival of a plant would not occur. They are as follows:

Carbon

Carbon is a key component of plant biomolecules that helps in the making of proteins, carbohydrates, nucleic acids, and other compounds. Carbon is present in almost all macronutrients.

Nitrogen

One of the most abundant and significant components in plants is nitrate, a form of nitrogen used by plants. It is a part of living cells and an essential part of all enzymes, proteins, nucleic acids, amino acids, and metabolic procedures that are involved in the synthesis of vitamins, development process, and transmission of energy. Nitrogen is responsible for the green pigmentation of plants by assisting the production of chlorophyll and influencing the fast growth of plants, and accelerating seed and fruit production, thus ameliorating the quality of leaves and fodder. The two most primary functions of a plant's body are photosynthesis and reproduction, and nitrogen plays an important role in both aspects.

Plants that contain less than 1% nitrogen are regarded as deficient in nitrogen. Insufficiency of nitrogen in plants causes stunted growth and weakening of leaves giving rise to wilted, yellow-colored pigments, depending upon the intensity of nitrogen inadequacy. Even an excessive amount of nitrogen poses a threat to the further evolution of plants. Thus, providing balanced and correct proportions of nitrogen is necessary. Several salts can provide nitrogen to plants like calcium nitrate, potassium nitrate, ammonium nitrate. Plants should be treated at the right time if they show any symptoms of deficiency. Ensure that the pH in the root zone ranges between 5.8 and 6.3.

Phosphorus

Phosphorus is another significant macromolecule that is very necessary for the plant's health and amalgamates phospholipids and nucleic acids. Phosphorus is required for the formation of sugar, starches, etc. It assists in accurate plant maturation by encouraging blooming and enhancing the growth of roots, flowers, and fruits. It helps in storing carbohydrates and provides strength for withstanding harsh environmental circumstances. It also helps perform respiration and contributes to photosynthesis, and conducts energy transport like conversion of solar energy into chemical energy through photophosphorylation and transformation of food energy into chemical energy by oxidative phosphorylation and cell division. When the plant is in the stage of germination, phosphorus is needed in more amounts than usual. There are varied kinds of plants that are grown hydroponically, yet they require more amount of phosphorus in their flowering stage than their vegetative state. The procedures of cell biosynthesis and nucleic acid are affected by the existence of phosphorus.

It is important to identify when a plant is deficient in phosphorus and treat it accordingly. When a plant has less than 0.01% P, immediate steps need to be taken before the plant shrivels and becomes thin and suppressed. Deficit symptoms generally appear on the older leaves first. The leaves turn bluish-green to deeper-reddish purple. In younger leaves, yellowish-green patches appear, showing signs of necrosis in an advanced stage. When P is present in excess amount, iron and zinc deficiency is caused. This problem can be managed by a 2% spray of diammonium phosphate and the correct dose of phosphorus besides other prime nutrients.

Potassium

Potassium is also one of the vital nutrients that plants need for proper growth and good supply in the upcoming days. Potassium bestows nourishment to plants by playing a major role in the escalation of proteins and necessary enzymes thus, contributing to early maturation and better fruit quality. Potassium also renders aids in regulating stomatal movements, helping maintain the osmotic pressure of plants, and retaining healthy water equilibrium in plants' bodies. A healthy plant tissue contains 1-5% potassium. It influences insect suppression too.

Deficiency symptoms of potassium mostly develop first in older leaves, causing necrosis, leading to brown and spindly leaf margins, reddening of leaves, and chlorosis in younger plants. Seeds and fruits that lack potassium shrinks in later days. Most importantly, the plant growth becomes slower than usual. Similarly, if the amount of potassium given to plants is in excess, it can hamper and threaten calcium and magnesium uptake. Especially you need to take utmost care and stay vigilant during the flowering stage of the plant. 1% muriate of potassium nitrate spray is recommended to deal with the dearth of potassium in plants.

Sulfur

Sulfur is a coenzyme compound and a significant ingredient of every plant as it assists in the manufacture of vitamins, enzymes, proteins, amino acids. It helps plants fight diseases and donates to the plant's proper upbringing, promoting the genesis of seeds and root growth. The area where sulfur plays a crucial role is the chlorophyll formation, thus contributing to photosynthesis.

When the sulfur content in a plant is less than 0.1 to 0.2%, the plant is considered to be S-deficient. Sulfur is an immobile nutrient and appears first in younger leaves. The deficiency symptoms of nitrogen and sulfur are almost similar that may cause confusion. Chlorosis is the most common symptom of inadequate sulfur. The deficiency of sulfur makes leaves yellowish. The plant stalks become thin, slender and growth becomes slow as well. The plants undergo maturity at a much later stage and cause premature dropping of leaves. Gypsum increases the sulfur levels in plants, and a 1% spray of water-soluble sulfur fertilizers is recommended.

Calcium

Calcium is an extremely vital nutrient that contributes to the formation of the plant cell wall and cell elongation. The right amount of calcium keeps all fungal problems and infections away. The absorption of all other nutrients depends on the calcium content of the plant. It provides strength and metabolism to endure issues that affect the evolution of a plant. Calcium in plants also helps prevent the effect of alkali salts and organic acids. Calcium plays a major role in controlling the transportation of nutrients and other enzyme functions.

Calcium deficiency in plants varies from 0.2 to 1%. This nutrient movement is very slow in plants, giving rise to defective growth, abnormal bud shapes, and abortion of blooms. The roots become stubby, which results in root death in later days, and even leaves experience mutation. Calcium deficient leaves, especially the newer leaves, become distorted, wilted, and possess an abnormal green coloration. The petioles break down, further causing necrosis, chlorosis, and overall leading to the deterioration of the plant health. At the same time, when calcium is present in excess in plants, it hampers the assimilation of magnesium and potassium. Gypsum, superphosphate, and dolomitic lime are some immensely important sources of calcium.

Magnesium

Magnesium is a vital part of the chlorophyll and essential for the photosynthetic process. It helps in activating many enzyme purposes required for growth. Nutrients like magnesium and other micronutrients contribute to the ionic stability of plants. A proper amount of magnesium must be given to a plant in the flowering stage because a lack of this nutrient may hinder the synthesis of energy in plants.

Plants that have less than 0.01% of magnesium are regarded as Mg deficient. It usually appears on older leaves. They either become whitish or yellowish in color, and symptoms include patches on the leaf surface with smaller sized and upward curling of leaves, scorched margins, interveinal chlorosis with a tinge of orange, purple and reddish color in some final products. The development of buds is hugely affected by Mg deficiency. This issue can be solved by detecting the deficiency at the correct time and offering the plants the right proportion of hydroponic nutrients that have plenty of magnesium.

Growing plants through this hydroponic system of using only nutrients has become convenient over time, as it not only provides good nourishment to plants but is also less time-consuming. The roots of the plants are always soaked in fine nutrients, helping in plant maturation with increased and quality yield in a shorter period. Gaining knowledge about the particular nutrients is vital because their deficiency needs to be appropriately treated to elude stunted growth and cell death.

Setting Up Appropriate Lighting

Green salad plant under LED grow light

People with insufficient outdoor space and the desire to grow their food often prefer hydroponics as their hobby. The entire world knows that the perfect source of lighting to grow plants is nothing other than the sun. But, if you face certain situations when you are unable to rely on this ideal source completely, artificial lighting works wonders in such cases. The artificial lighting form is capable of supplying the most favorable lighting conditions to your indoor plants. Apart from that, you will be able to select the suitable light spectrum that you are willing to give your plants.

I am quite sure that being a beginner, you might find the task of choosing proper lights that suits your system quite daunting. But you need not worry at all as you will come across a lot of alternatives. The light suitable for your system depends on your system's size and the kinds of plants. Some kinds of plants may prove to be more efficient or better than the other types.

Generally, every vegetable garden requires about four to six hours of sunlight (direct) regularly, followed by nearly ten hours of sunlight (indirect) or very bright light. While making the use of artificial lighting, you need to remember one simple thing that everything is similar to a normal outdoor garden. Your main goal will be imitating all the conditions of any normal garden. Thus, you are supposed to make a plan such that your system gets fourteen to sixteen hours of artificial bright light along with approximately ten to twelve hours of darkened phase per day. Now, remember or rather understand one thing very clearly. The darkened phase about which I have mentioned refers to complete darkness. This dark phase is equally essential, like the phase where light is required for the plants to grow rapidly and in a healthy manner. Now, you might be thinking that why is the dark phase important? It is because the plants go through rest and metabolism during this phase.

The schedule of lighting tends to become more specific and stricter for perennials. The calculation of the light and dark phases also needs to be done more accurately for both the vegetative and flowering stages of perennial plants. The simplest way of maintaining this schedule is by taking the help of an electric timer that is automatic by nature. It means such a timer will maintain the entire lighting schedule on your behalf. Many people might think that investing in an automatic timer is a waste of money. But it is just the opposite. It will prove to be a profitable investment as the growth of your plants may get stunted if they do not get the required amount of both phases. Besides this, the productivity rate of the plants may also get affected dramatically.

Lighting Needs Differ from One Plant to Another

Here, you need to understand one thing that the lighting requirement of all plants is not the same. Many plants are there that love a prolonged period of daylight, and others are there that favor shorter periods. Now, if your garden consists of plants belonging to both the above-mentioned varieties, then you are supposed to customize their lighting schedule in such a manner so that it fulfills both the requirements. You can customize the schedule without any hassle just by using an automatic timer. The best part is that you can adjust the schedule according to your needs when your garden starts evolving.

Short Day Plants

These plants prefer a long dark period and shorter exposure to light for performing photosynthesis and producing flowers. If by chance, you expose such plants to bright light for more than twelve hours per day, then they will not produce flowers. Here are the examples of some short-day plants – cauliflower, poinsettias, strawberries, and chrysanthemums, etc. Thus, if any one of you are growing plants belonging to this category using the hydroponic setup, you just need to build up a suitable environment imitating the cycle of a short day.

Long Day Plants

Long-day plants are those plants that have a preference of about eighteen hours of bright daylight each day. A few plants falling in this particular category include lettuce, turnips, potatoes, spinach, and wheat. So, if you are planning to grow such plants utilizing the hydroponic setup, you have to imitate the cycle of a long day for them.

Day Neutral Plants

If you are looking for plants with the highest flexibility, then these are the ones. Apart from being flexible, day-neutral plants can be grown very easily. The best thing about these plants is they will produce fruits without depending on the amount of light they are exposed to. Some day-neutral plants are eggplant, roses, corn, and rice.

What Should You Look for in a Grow Light?

Before choosing a specific grow light for a hydroponic garden, you need to look for certain things. Here, in this section, we will be discussing all those factors –

Light Spectrum Output

When a plant goes through the vegetative phase, it requires light of an extremely short wavelength. It is because the light of such wavelength boosts or stimulates the plant's overall growth in its vegetative stage. This wavelength is also ideal for photosynthesis. Mostly, plants reflect the light spectrum that ranges between 480-580 nanometers. Hence, this light remains unutilized. In comparison, a light spectrum that is above 580 nanometers assists in speeding up the growth of stems. It is even helpful in both flowering and chlorophyll production. In other words, the blue and red spectrum is used by the plants at the time of development, reflecting back the green spectrum.

So, now we understand that red light promotes flowering, and blue one promotes vegetation. Thus, if you need optimal indoor lighting, the best option is to use grow lights emitting blue and red light mostly. You must also observe the output of light energy for getting the finest yield from your garden. Instead of purchasing two individual grow lights, you can go for specially designed LED lights for cost-cutting.

Light Intensity Output

In simple words, the quantity of light energy getting emitted per unit is termed light intensity. The unit used for measuring a bulb's brightness is lumens. But, a lot of people confuse lumens with watts. You must understand one thing that Watts is used for measuring energy. Here is the formula for measuring the light intensity = Light output / (Distance)^2

Suppose you have taken an HID light with 120,000 lumens of brightness and kept it at a distance of 4 feet from your plant. Hence, your plant will receive the light of only 7,500 lumens. Keeping the formula in mind, the light intensity will decrease drastically if the distance between the light and the plant is increased. So, if the size of your garden is small, you can purchase those bulbs that have lighter intensity.

Price Range

You must consider the grow light's price range. Usually, the price range of starter bulbs is $20-$50. But, if you are willing to select those that are expensive, then the cost may escalate to $300.

Types of Grow Lights

Close Up of Fluorescent Tubes

In this part, we will get to know about the different kinds of lighting systems one can apply in their hydroponic setup.

Fluorescent Grow Lights

Considering the price range, it is doubtless that the fluorescent grow lights are very much economical and exist for many years. Using these lights is of great advantage as they will not harm your plants even if the distance between the plant and the light is less. It is because these grow lights produce little heat. But a disadvantage comes with this advantage too. Here it is – these grow lights prove to be less strong for some plants.

T5 Lighting Fixtures

You need to have knowledge regarding the T5 lighting fixtures. These fixtures are available in two particular variations – the first one being the 4ft length, the second one being the 2ft length. Certain fixtures are there that have the potential of holding six or twelve lighting tubes altogether.

T5 Bulbs

Nowadays, people are investing in these bulbs because they provide the opportunity of covering various types of color temperature. These bulbs are available in a total number of 3 output ranges – 1) the NO or Normal Output, 2) the H.O. or High Output, and lastly 3) the VHO or Very High Output. If you are a beginner, then I would prefer to recommend the High Output variety.

HID Lights

In hydroponic systems, HID or high-intensity discharge lights are widely used as the bulbs of these lights are extremely large along with high-intensity range. HID lights are of two types. They are –

- HPS – The light that is produced by the HPS or High-Pressure Sodium lights is of the red/orange spectrum. So, if your garden plants are in the flowering phase at present, then use these lights.

- M.H. – The light that is produced by the Metal Halide bulbs is of the bluer spectrum. So, when the plants go through the vegetative stage, you can select these M.H. lights.

If you desire to install these lights in the hydroponic system, then the installation of certain other parts is also required for smooth functioning. These are –

- *Reflectors* – Reflectors are highly essential while utilizing HID lights. These parts are attached just above the lights. Its job is directing light towards your plants.

- *Ballast* – This part of your lighting system will help in switching on the bulb. It even plays the role of assuring that the electricity flow is perfect. Basically, ballasts are of two types – magnetic ballast and digital ballast. The first type possesses a coil and a condenser which help in regulating the power. The other ballast is more effective and cost-efficient than the other one.

But you need to be aware of one thing while using the HID lights. It is – if the distance between the plants and the lights is not proper, your plants may get burned because of the heat of those lights.

LED Lights

Diode strip. LED lights tape

Usage of LED lights in hydroponic systems is comparatively new. Though they are more expensive than the two options mentioned above, they can still offer great benefits. Not only are they energy-efficient, but they also emit more light compared to the other alternatives. The best part is that excessive heat is not generated from these lights, which will help you protect your plants from getting burnt. Moreover, additional ballasts are not required for operating these lights.

Your only task is plugging the lights in the sockets and waiting to enjoy the productivity. The LED lights can be adjusted to the specific color temperature needed by your plant. It is because LED lights offer a diverse light spectrum.

The grow lights about which I have discussed above are the primary ones. You can now use induction lighting as better technology is arriving in the market almost every day. You may also look into the double-ended lighting system. It consists of tubes that are double-ended along with HPS bulbs. Other than these lights, sulfur plasma lights are also available that help to replicate the sun's effect. But these lights are not so commonly used as they are still getting developed.

Every single grow light has different pros and cons, and it's your responsibility to judge their characteristics based on your requirement for choosing the grow light appropriate for your lovely hydroponic garden.

Chapter 4
A Step-by-Step Guide to Build Your Own Hydroponic Garden

Now let us move on to how you can build your hydroponic setup in the easiest way possible. In this chapter, I will walk you through some basic concepts like the basic equipment you need, things you should consider before building the garden, and finally, move on to some DIY setups and how you can build them in a step-by-step manner.

So, without any further ado, let's dig right in!

Things You Will Need to Build Your Hydroponic Setup

The first step to building your hydroponic garden is to know what equipment you need, and in this section, we will cover it in detail.

Grow Tray

Organic hydroponic vegetable grows with LED Light Indoor farm

The first and most essential thing you need is a grow tray. It is basically a container where, as the name suggests, you grow the plants. They can either be designed to hold only one plant or multiple, depending on your setup and the plant that you are growing. In some of these trays, the water can drain out to avoid accumulation through the leach valves present in them. On the other hand, there are also grow trays where the purpose is to hold some form of growing media like clay pebbles, perlite, coco coir, and so on. And lastly, you will also find grow trays where pots are kept, and the plants are then established in these pots with the growing media.

You might also find the word hydroponic tray being used in place of a grow tray in some places.

Hydroponic Gardening

Whenever it comes to a hydroponic system, the type, size, and shape of grow trays differ to a great extent. The specific type of hydroponic gardening you have decided to do will ultimately determine the type of grow tray you need.

But if we talk about it generally, then hydroponic trays are built to accommodate the plants properly and give them enough space to grow their roots. They are usually shallow, rectangular, or somewhat long in shape. Grow trays are not as such used in aeroponic systems and are mostly reserved for different types of hydroponic systems.

Let us talk about grow trays in the flood and drain system. You will either see cups and pots containing the plants arranged on the tray, or you might also find the plants in the grow tray in a growing medium. Irrespective of the scenario, at regular intervals, a nutrient solution will be pumped into the grow tray. This ensures that the plants can get their desired nutrition before the nutrient solution is again pumped out.

On the other hand, in a run to waste system, the grow tray is not placed on a flat area but rather on a sloped surface. Several drainage holes are made along the lower edge, and then the grow tray is filled with the desired growing medium. On the top of the entire system, nutrients and water are both added from time to time in a periodical fashion. Both of these things seep inside and then ultimately drain out after a certain point of time through the bottom of the grow tray.

Then, there is the deep-water culture system where the nutrition solution is placed below, and all the plants are suspended. The mixture is refreshed and oxygenated regularly. In this type of system, most of the time, you will not find any grow tray at all, and even if you find it, it might look something very different. The most common alternative that is used is a sealed bucket.

Reservoir

Irrespective of the type of hydroponic system you are going to build, one of its major parts will be the reservoir. As you know, hydroponics is all about water, and the reservoir is where you store it. But it does not only contain the water but also the nutrients along with it that promote healthy growth in your plants. In some systems, the nutrient solution from the reservoir is passively delivered to the plants. Whereas in some systems, the nutrient content is delivered actively.

Let us look at the functions of the reservoir in brief –

- For starters, the reservoir is responsible for storing the nutrient solution and then circulating it to all the plants in the system.

- It is because of the reservoir that you get the container to prepare the nutrient solution in. In an ideal situation, it is advised that you have the provision for two reservoirs. This will ensure that while you are using one of the reservoirs in the system itself, you can use the spare one to keep the next batch of the nutrient solution prepared before the present one is all used up.

- You can easily adjust and monitor the pH value of the solution because of the reservoir. With a change in the temperature and concentration of the nutrient solution, the first and foremost thing that is affected is the pH. And if you want the plants in your hydroponic system to remain healthy, maintaining the right pH level should be on your priority list. With each pH level, the plant's ability to take up nutrients also changes. Your plants might be facing nutrient deficiency or nutrient toxicity simply because of a change in the pH levels. You can either use a pH meter or a pH test kit to measure the pH in the reservoir. The rate of change in pH is considerably reduced in systems that have larger reservoirs.

- The concentration of the nutrition solution can be adjusted without hassle because it is present in the reservoir. The concentration of a nutrient solution never stays constant. There are several factors because of which it keeps changing, and the first and foremost of which is evaporation. In fact, if the hydroponic system is left unattended for a long time, the worst thing that is going to happen is that the solution will become extremely concentrated, making it difficult for the plants to take up any nutrients at all. Thus, you must keep adjusting and checking this concentration level on a periodic basis. An electronic EC meter is sufficient for the job of checking the concentration.

- Similarly, because of the reservoir, you can adjust the temperature of the nutrient solution as well. If you want your plants to be healthy, maintaining your nutrient solution's right temperature is a crucial task. The ideal temperature in most cases is in the range of 20-24 degrees Celsius. Maintaining this level of temperature is often easier for people living in temperate climates. But it becomes more challenging when the place you live in has a higher or much lower temperature range than the ideal. A perfect hack to prevent rapid temperature changes is to get an insulated nutrient reservoir.

Air Pump

I know that at times you might feel all of these details are so overwhelming, but if you take it day by day, things will start to seem easier. Air pumps are not required in all systems. The ones where the roots of your plants are almost fully submerged in water are the systems where you need an air pump. But in the case of aeroponics or the Kratky method, where the roots of the plants are mostly kept exposed, you don't need an air pump.

But why are these air pumps needed in the first place? In order to make your plants survive, you need to give them a sufficient amount of oxygen. The parts of the plant that remain above, that is, the green parts, perform photosynthesis and fulfill their oxygen requirement. But have you thought about the roots? They need oxygen too, and they get it either from water or soil. Now, here the air pumps perform their role by enriching the water with oxygen.

Air Stone

Air stones are used for the very same reason as air pumps. If you have had an aquarium in the house, then you already know what air stones look like and what their function is. But we are going to quickly go over it in this section. Air stones also aid in the formation of small air bubbles that help in the oxygenation of the water. Air stones are usually placed right at the bottom of your reservoir. When they produce these little bubbles, the bubbles rise up and touch the roots of the hydroponic plants, thus providing them with oxygen.

You need the air pump to operate these air stones. In some cases, you might even set a timer so that the bubbles will be released in regular intervals. It is better if you keep the air stone soaked in water before putting it to use.

Growing Medium

The growing medium is another obvious requirement of any hydroponic system. It consists of different types of materials in which you will be growing your plants. In traditional gardening, you are limited to only soil as your growing medium, but it is not so in hydroponics.

Your plants need oxygen and moisture for growth, and both of these things will be provided to them by the growing medium. We have already covered the growing media in depth in Chapter 3.

Monitoring Equipment

Some factors in a hydroponic system need to be monitored regularly for optimum growth of plants. Two of the main controlling systems that you should have are conductivity controllers and pH controllers. When there is something wrong with the nutrient concentration in the reservoir, for example, if it becomes too high, the conductivity controller will take care of it by diluting the nutrients. Similarly, the pH controller will maintain an optimum level of pH in the solution.

Fertilizer and Nutrient Solution

Just like you need to apply fertilizers to the soil in the case of traditional gardening, hydroponics requires a nutrient solution. Every plant has a different requirement when it comes to nutrients, and thus, the nutrient solution of your setup should be made accordingly. We have already talked about the basic nutrients in Chapter 3.

Lighting

For proper growth of your hydroponic plants, you need to give them the right lighting conditions. Both the duration and intensity of light play a significant role here. If the plants do not get a sufficient amount of light, they will not have strong stems and develop somewhat spindly and weak stems. On the other hand, the leaves will fail to develop fully in the absence of optimal lighting conditions.

Consequently, if you give the plant the light it requires, it will perform photosynthesis the way it should and utilize the nutrients given to it in the right manner. Thus, without the right or adequate amount of lighting, you will never be able to grow the plant to its full potential.

Artificial lighting has developed to a great extent in today's world, and we have covered this topic in Chapter 3 itself.

Timer

When you are building a hydroponic system, a timer is also one of the most essential pieces of equipment. A timer is often used in the light access control or submersible pump control. All plants don't require the same duration of light. And you might not always be at home to control the lighting. So, an easier solution is to set the lights on a timer. In this way, your lighting schedule will remain perfect without any hassle.

Systems like the ebb and flow systems need a timer because the nutrient solution has to be controlled. It needs to flood the grow bed from time to time, and there is a fixed time interval for that. It is not humanly possible for anyone to constantly stand in front of the hydroponic system and maintain this. Thus, a timer is a much easier alternative.

Water Pump

There are two types of water pumps used in hydroponic systems – submersible and inline. Since, in most cases, the water has to be vertically pumped up to reach the roots of the plants against gravity, a water pump is required. The size of the water pump you need will greatly depend on the vertical distance that the water has to cover. So, experts always advise you to get a water pump that claims to perform better than what you need. In this way, you can rule out any chances of an underperforming pump.

So, these are some of the basic things you will need to build a hydroponic setup. Now, let us move on to some of the factors you need to keep in mind.

Factors to Keep in Mind Before Setting Up Your Hydroponic Garden

Over the past few years, hydroponics has garnered quite the attention. But before you dive right into buying your equipment from the local store, there are some factors that you need to judge for maximum yield.

Consider the Space You Have

First, decide where you want to build your hydroponic system and how much space you have there. Then, you need to add to it the size of the hydroponic system that you plan to build. You can build a hydroponic system easily in your home in spaces like greenhouses, spare rooms, garages, and also warehouses. Well, in short, you can grow your plants hydroponically anywhere where you will have complete control over the growing environment.

If you already have such a space in mind, it is imperative that you first form the layout of your hydroponic setup in that space. While doing this, you should remember that it is not only about the size of the system itself, but many other factors need to be kept in mind, for example, the prep areas, refrigeration units, storage areas, walkways, fertigation system, and water tanks. All of these things should be taken into your consideration right from the stage of planning; otherwise, later on, it will all seem messed up. In fact, people who don't think about these from the early stages often end up overcrowding the overall space, which, in turn, makes it difficult for them to move around.

But if you don't have an existing space where you can build the hydroponic system, you will need to find one. In that case, the first thing to keep in mind is your production needs. In short, think long-term. Are you considering hydroponics as only a hobby? If so, then you will not have to think about things like expansion. For people who only want to do it as a hobby, you can find just about any controlled space or build a greenhouse if your budget permits.

However, people who do not want to stick to it as a hobby and want to take it to a commercial level will need much more space and also keep in mind that they will have to expand in the future. For such a scenario, the best thing to do would be to build the setup in commercial growing facilities or greenhouses. Don't start with a lot of crops in the beginning. Start small and then work your way up from there.

If you want your venture to succeed, correct planning in the early stages is a must. You cannot afford to make costly mistakes, and planning it out will help you prevent such a situation from occurring.

Consider the Type of Plants You Want to Grow

The next most important thing to consider before building your hydroponic garden is what type of plants you will be growing. Do you know why it is essential? Certain types of plants require the gardener to implement certain types of methods, which will dictate your entire setup.

Let me give you an example. Suppose you want to grow tomatoes. For these, the NFT hydroponic system would definitely not be the suitable choice. Thus, if you decide the type of plants you want to grow right from the beginning, you can also buy the right equipment without wasting any money. You don't have to do too many alterations later on, saving you a lot of time and energy.

On the other hand, if you are doing hydroponic gardening as a commercial grower, then the type of plants you want to grow should factor in the market demand as well. If the market in which you are going to sell is already an established one, it will be easy for you to find out which crops are in greater demand and decide which plants to grow.

Here is an example – let us say that you want to grow lettuce, but the market that you will be supplying already has lettuce in adequate amounts. Thus, the demand for lettuce will be quite low. Thus, if you still want to continue with lettuce production, you can do so on a small scale. On the other hand, if you decide on selling cucumbers in the same market, you will have far greater demand. In fact, it might so happen that the people are demanding the cucumbers to such a great extent that you can't keep up with it. So, if you are doing it on a commercial scale, understanding these demand and supply concepts will help you understand how big of a system you need to build.

If the market you are trying to break into is relatively new to you, approach customers and talk to them. Know what they are looking for and assess their demands. In this way, simple research can help you understand what is in most demand among the potential consumers.

Keep Your Budget in Mind

Have you thought about how much money you plan to invest in this hydroponic project? If you haven't thought about it yet, it is high time that you do now.

When you decide your budget at an early stage, you can assess which systems are in your budget and which systems need to be ruled out. Don't worry if your budget is tight because every budget will be able to accommodate a particular type of hydroponic system in it.

The budget factor will obviously vary from one person to another. If your ultimate aim is to turn your hydroponic production into a commercial-scale business, then the investment in your setup will also be way more. Your average ROI or return on investment will be around three to four years. But if you plan to sell fruits and veggies on a stand by the road, a small setup would be enough, and naturally, you can start your business with a much lower investment cost. If you take my advice, I'll tell you to start small, especially if you are a beginner.

Irrespective of how much research you have performed on this subject, you should get to know the market first by producing on a small scale. There is a huge difference between researching and actually selling something. If your business runs well, then you can always consider expanding, but until then, there is no need for you to invest a chunk of your savings into this.

Think About How Much Time You Can Invest

Are you doing this simply as a hobby, or do you plan to start a full-time business through hydroponic gardening?

The system mostly overlooks the actual process of crop production, but there are so many other things that need your supervision. This includes pest management, cleaning, transplanting, pruning, and harvesting. In fact, if you think about it carefully, you'll see that the only traditional task that you don't have to do actively in hydroponics is watering. If you don't want the entire thing to be too overwhelming for you, you should start with a small setup.

Another important thing to keep in mind is that when you are starting your endeavor in the initial days, it is quite natural for a person to pay more attention to the setup. You will be spending more time behind it by looking closely at all the changes. Once you have traversed a certain distance on your learning curve, you will slowly want to settle down for a simpler routine. However, it is not easy for a person to reach that point. Every day, you will be going through new stages of learning, experimentation, and observation. So, it is imperative that before you plan your hydroponic system, don't forget the time constraints. Keep in mind that certain hydroponic systems require more of your time than others.

DIY Hydroponic Systems

Hydroponic farm

In this section, I will give you step-by-step instructions to build some DIY hydroponic setups.

Simple Wick System

You already learned about the wick system and how it works in Chapter 2. Here we are going to build a very simple form of it using very basic materials. So, without any further ado, let's get started.

Materials You Need –

- A soda bottle – 1 or 2 liters

- Two-thirds cup of coco coir
- String or cotton rope – 6-24 inches in length
- Four cups of water
- One-third cup of perlite
- Four lettuce seeds
- One tablespoon of plant food
- One ruler
- One marker
- One craft knife
- One cutting mat
- One hammer or drill with nails

Steps to Follow:

Step 1 – Gather all the materials you need from the list above.

Step 2 – Make a marking with a permanent marker at three inches counted from the bottom of the bottle. To make sure that the marking is even, you can make the markings on both sides of the bottle and then join the markings with a line. Now, follow that line and cut the top portion of the bottle with the craft knife. Then, you have to check the fit. So, take the top cut portion and carefully place it on the bottom portion.

Step 3 – Next, it is time to create the wick. There is basically more than one way in which you can complete this step. The easiest way is to get your hands on an electric drill and then make a hole into the cap of the bottle. And the second method is to do it the old-fashioned way using a hammer and a nail. The size of the hole in the cap can be altered based on your preference.

Step 4 – The next task is to place the wick in position. You might have to loop your string in some cases, but this will depend on the string's thickness. Take the string and cut off 12 inches from it. Loop it if necessary. Now, insert the string through the hole in the cap. Insert it in a way that half of it remains inside the bottle, and the other half remains outside. Inside the cap, make a knot in the string. Make sure the knot is extremely close to the cap.

Step 5 – Take the suggested amounts of perlite and coco coir and mix them well. In the top portion of the bottle, add this growing media. Now keep the top portion of the bottle aside. Take four cups of water and add the plant food to it. Mix well. Mark on the bottle the height you want the water to achieve while ensuring that the wick is submerged. Then, fill the water into the bottle up to the mark. Place the top portion of the bottle on the bottom cut portion, and your setup is complete.

Step 6 – Lastly, all you need to do is plant the seeds in the growing media. The depth of sowing of the seeds varies from one plant to another. So, follow the instructions mentioned in the packet. Set the system under the sun, and soon, you will be able to watch your plants grow!

Deep Water Culture Setup

A DIY deep water culture setup is not a hassle to build, and with the proper guidance, you can build it in very quickly. Read on to find out how.

Materials You Need:

- A tote with a lid – here, you need to make sure that the material used to make the tote is strong (for example, sturdy plastic)
- Clay pebbles
- Net pots – 3-4 inch in size
- Aquarium air pump
- Check valve
- Air hose

- Air stone
- Drill bit
- Hole saw kit
- Drill
- Marker

Steps to Follow:

Step 1 – The first thing that you need to do is make holes for the air hose and the net pots. But before that, decide on the positioning of the net pots. The positioning will be pretty easy when your system consists of a lesser number of plants, like only five or so. The best method would be to set your net pots in the exact position you want them on the lid and then use a marker to mark those areas. The holes can be easily cut out with the hole saw. The size of the holes should be perfect to simply allow the net pots to fit in and not fall through.

Step 2 – At the end of the lid, drill a hole. This will be used for the air hose. Most of the work is completed. Now, all is left is to assemble the system.

Step 3 – The task of providing oxygen to your plants lies with the air system. The air hose has to be cut up to a length that will easily pass from the reservoir to the pump. The air stone needs to be connected to one end of your air hose, and the other end will have to be pushed through the hole you made on the lid. To maintain proper airflow, keep in mind that the check valve has to go the right way in.

Step 4 – Take the air hose and cut off a few more inches. This part will help you connect to the check valve. Now, connect the air hose to the air pump through the open end. Congratulations, you have successfully completed the assembly of your setup.

Step 5 – Prepare the nutrient solution. Once you have added the required amount of nutrient solution into the tote, wait for fifteen minutes. After that, check the pH and adjust it if necessary.

Step 6 – Finally, all you need to do now is add your plants. You can use Rockwool to start your seedlings, and when they are big enough, you can plant them in the system. Add Hydroton in the nets and then carefully place the seedling in it. Use clay pebbles around the plant so that they reach the level of the plant. And, your DWC setup is done!

Ebb and Flow System

Here, I will show you how to build a small yet dependable ebb and flow hydroponic unit in a very easy and quick process.

Hydroponic Gardening

Materials You Need:

- Black colored tote bin with lid – anything between 16-20 gallons
- Snap topper tote bin – transparent (30 qt.) – make sure this fits properly on top of the tote bin
- Aquarium air pump
- Timer
- 5-inch air stone
- T connector
- Six feet of airline tubing
- Small bag of perlite
- Four units of 8" flower pots
- Submersible pond pump – small – 120 gph
- Black colored irrigation tubing – approximately 18 inches long with an inner diameter of half an inch
- Small bag of LECA and one brick of coco coir
- 3/8 inches spade or regular drill bit

- 1-1/4 inches hole saw
- Power drill
- Fill and drain fitting set
- Marker

Steps to Follow:

Step 1 – At the middle portion of your snap topper tray, make two holes, and each hole should be approximately 1-1/4" in size. Use sandpaper to smooth out the edges. The holes should be made in such a way that all four pots should fit around them properly.

Step 2 – Now, on top of the lid of your black tote, place the clear tray. Use a marker to mark the center of each of these holes that you made in Step 1 on the black tote lid. Then, you have to make two holes on the black tote lid exactly where you marked. These holes should also be 1-1/4" in size. In short, the holes should be properly aligned.

Step 3 – On either side of the black lid, two more holes have to be made of the same size as above. Through one of these holes, you will pass the bubbler tubing and the pump plug. And through the other one, you will add the nutrient solution when required and check the solution's level.

Step 4 – Now, take the two drain fittings, and place them in the holes that you made in the center of the transparent tray. On the underside, the rubber gasket should be present. You need not use any tools to tighten – using your hand is enough. In the overflow tube, place only one extension.

Step 5 – Let us now move on to the plumbing process. On top of the water pump outlet fitting, you need to place the half-inch irrigation tubing. The fit should be snug. So, if it's needed, you can always use a zip tie to secure it in place.

Step 6 – Take the clear tray and place it on top of the black lid in a way that they fit in place. Most importantly, the holes should align on top of each other perfectly.

Step 7 – Take the black tubing and trim it to a length that will ensure that the pump can be placed at the bottom of the black bin, which will act as your reservoir. Now insert the tubing into the shorter drain tube and ensure a proper fit. The tubing assembly should not be loose or slipping away. You can use a zip tie if needed. At the bottom of the black bin, add the bubbler stone. Then, the pump plug and the airline tubing should be passed through the side ports that you had drilled in the previous steps. Now arrange the tray assembly on top of each other so that they fit in place.

Step 8 – Now, add water into the black bin, approximately 10 gallons. Choose the nutrient concentrate you want and mix it. Wait for fifteen minutes and then check the pH. If it's not what you need it to be, adjust the pH. Then, plug in the pump and the bubbler to check whether there is any leakage.

Step 9 – Take your seedlings and plant them in the pot. Make sure they have been set well into the growing medium. Remember that you have to do the seedlings elsewhere because the seeds cannot be started directly in an ebb and flow system.

Step 10 – Set the timer for the water pump and set it to fill the system thrice a day, and each fill cycle should be for fifteen minutes only. At night, allow the plants to rest. However, the bubbler pump should be kept on all day and night. This ensures that the nutrient solution is well oxygenated.

Now that you have a comprehensive idea of how to build your own hydroponic system, we will move on to the next chapter, where I will tell you all about the plants that you can grow using hydroponics.

Chapter 5
What Are the Best Plants for a Hydroponic System?

If you ask which plants can be grown hydroponically, then the answer is "any plant." You can literally grow any plant hydroponically, but the thing is, some will not survive, and some won't be able to reach up to their full potential. Some plants are a little harder to grow in a Hydroponic system. It doesn't mean that it is impossible, but you must avoid those in your first attempt if you are a beginner.

What to Grow and What Not to Grow?

In case you have limited space, it is advised that you avoid corn, pumpkins, melons, squash, etc. Growing them in a narrow area is not impossible but maintaining them and taking care of them becomes troublesome and challenging. Yields for these plants are not good if grown in a small space. It is advised that you avoid certain deep-rooted vegetables. Examples include carrots, turnips, and potatoes. This is because while growing these crops, you will be needing a substrate that has high depth and enough length for supporting those roots.

Moreover, these plants give better yields when grown on soil, compared to when they are grown in a soilless Hydroponic system. In case you have a large growing place like a patio or a greenhouse, you will be able to set up an advanced system. This will allow you to grow deep-rooted veggies, sizable plants, and the ones that are hard to grow otherwise. You can play around and experiment with different plants if you have access to a growing area like that.

Here are some plants that are perfect for growing in a hydroponic system.

Vegetables

There are a lot of vegetables that you can grow in a water-based system. A lot of them are those that can also be grown in a garden. Some of them are only for growing in a limited and confined space. Remember that if you are providing enough light to your plant and feeding it properly, it will grow. If you want to grow large plants like tomatoes, you can use clay pebbles. The roots will be able to have a firm hold because of these clay pebbles.

Here are some vegetables that are ideal for growing in a hydroponic system:

Lettuce

Lettuce

It is one of the most common vegetables found in every household. It goes perfectly with your sandwiches and salads. They have a fast growth rate, and it is very simple to take care of them. Lettuces can be grown in almost any type of Hydroponic system like Flow, Ebb, NFT, etc. If you are planning to begin growing plants in a hydroponic system, you can start with this first because the process is simple. Cool temperatures are ideal for them, and their pH should be somewhere between 6 and 7. Their growing time is usually within 30 days or even less.

Tomatoes

Tomatoes on the Vine

You can grow both cherry tomatoes and regular tomatoes in a Hydroponic system. Tomato is a very basic ingredient that is used in almost every meal. When you no longer want to consume tomatoes that are commercially grown, you can try to grow them in your home in a soilless system. Hot temperatures are ideal for growing tomatoes, and they need lots of light to flourish. In case you are planning to grow them inside your home, you should buy grow lights so that you can provide them the light they require. The pH should be between 5.5 – 6.5.

Radishes

Bunch fresh radish with cut

Radishes can grow very nicely both in a Hydroponic system and in soil. You can expect to harvest them after one month. Cool temperatures are ideal for growing radishes. You can purchase seeds and start growing in your Hydroponic system. No special lighting needs to be provided by you in case of growing radishes. They take around three to seven days to grow. Their ideal temperature varies between 10 to 18 degrees Celsius, and their ideal pH is between 6.0 – 7.0.

Kale

Fresh green organic kale

If you are someone who is very health-conscious, then the best thing for you to grow in your hydroponic system is kale. Kales are delectable and are very nutritious. It is a very healthy vegetable, and nothing can be better than being able to grow them and having them in abundance in your home. Growing kale in Hydroponic systems has been going on for a long time now. So, you can be 100% sure that they are going to flourish well in your Hydroponic system as well. Moderate temperatures are ideal for them to grow. Their maintenance is super simple, and the ideal pH should be between 5.5 – 6.5.

Cucumbers

Fresh picked cucumbers

Cucumber is a very commonly found vegetable that is grown mostly in commercial greenhouses. You can also grow them in your home hydroponic system. Their growth rate is very fast, and they produce good yields. You may get confused while choosing the type because there are so many to choose from. You can go for the Lebanese cucumbers, or the seedless and elongated variants of the European cucumbers, or the American slicers. Each of these is going to flourish nicely in your home hydroponic system. Cucumbers are warm plants, and they require ample amounts of high temperatures and light to grow well. Their pH should be between 5.5 – 6.0.

Spinaches

Portion of fresh Spinach

Spinaches also have a very fast growth rate and are well-suited for your home Hydroponic system. Although they can be grown in almost every type of Hydroponic system, it is recommended that you use the Nutrient Film technique since it works the best for them. In case you opt for some other technique, just make sure that the soil you are using is duly oxygenated and is rich in nutrients. For growing spinach, you are going to need a comparatively lesser amount of water. You can purchase seeds and grow them from scratch in your home hydroponic system. Usually, they take around 40 days to grow fully. The temperature should be warm, and the pH should be between 6.0 – 7.5. If you are growing sweet spinach in your home hydroponic system, you need to make sure that the temperature is between 65 and 72 degrees Fahrenheit. If the temperature is lower than this, then the plant will take longer to grow. There are a lot of options to choose from, like the Bloomsdale, Red Cardinals, Savoys, and the Catalinas. Growing them is super-easy and caring for them is really simple too.

Beans

Group of beans and lentils

It is another good option for your home's hydroponic system, and the maintenance is simple too. Beans go with almost every meal, and it is very convenient to have them in your home in abundance. This will ensure that you can use them whenever you want. The types you can choose from are pinto beans, pole beans, green beans, and string beans. Lima, an uncommon type of bean, can also be grown in your home hydroponic system. You will need a trellis if you are planning to grow string beans or pole beans. This will be ensuring that your plant gets the support when they need it. It will take almost 3 to 8 days to germinate and another 6 to 8 weeks for harvesting. After harvesting, the beans can be grown for another 3 – 4 months. Warm temperatures are ideal for growing them, and the pH should be between 6.0 – 6.3.

Peppers

Colourful bell peppers

Bell peppers are an excellent option to be grown in your home hydroponic system. If you are growing bell peppers in your home, then please make sure they don't reach their full height. For ensuring this, the plant can be pinched and pruned at 7 or 8 inches. It will be responsible for spurring their growth and making them fuller and bigger. The Deep-Water Culture technique is the most suitable technique when it comes to growing bell peppers. If not, then go for the Flow technique or the Ebb technique. Their growing time is around 90 days, and their pH should be between 6.0 – 6.5. Your bell peppers should get an ample amount of light to flourish. Eighteen hours of continuous, uninterrupted light is ideal for them. The light rack can also be raised when your bell peppers start to grow. The plant should be six inches away from the light. There are a lot of types to choose from, like Yolo, Vidi, or the Ace variants. Warm temperatures are ideal for growing bell peppers.

Celery

Fresh celery stalks

It is a very healthy vegetable that has a great texture and a lot of flavors. They can be grown in the Ebb and Flow hydroponic system. You need to ensure that the roots are not submerged and the stalks are wet. The ideal pH should be between 5.7 – 6.0.

Fruits

There are quite some fruits that you can grow in a hydroponic system. If you love to consume health-friendly foods, you probably eat a lot of fruits. Instead of going to the market every time and spending loads of money on fruits, you can just grow them at your home and eat them whenever you want.

Here are some fruits ideal for growing in a Hydroponic system:

Strawberries

Fresh strawberries fallen out of a wooden basket outdoors

If you are a strawberry lover, you might find yourself complaining about the seasonal nature of this fruit. It remains unavailable most times of the year and is also quite costly (although the price varies from place to place). If you are growing strawberries in a Hydroponic system, then you can grow them at any time of the year. Harvesting strawberries is very convenient and simple. It is recommended to grow strawberries in the Ebb and Flow system. If you want, you can also go for the Deep-Water Culture technique using a nutrient film. Their growth time is somewhat around 60 days. Warm temperatures are ideal for them, and the pH should be between 5.5 – 6.2. In case you want to grow strawberries in your home hydroponic system, it is recommended that you don't buy strawberry seeds. This is because they will take a couple of years to fully flourish with berries fully. Instead, purchase cold-stored seeds that are at a growing stage. Brighton, Tioga, and Chandler are the best options when it comes to strawberries.

Blueberries

Fresh blueberry with drops of water in wooden bowl

Blueberries are a rich source of vitamins and an amazing choice for growing in a Hydroponic system.

Their growth rate is a little slower compared to the strawberries. In some cases, the plants take a few months to bear the first fruit. The NFT technique is the best for growing blueberries, Warm temperatures are ideal for growing them, and the pH should be between 4.5 – 6.0. It is recommended not to grow them from seeds. Instead, go for transplants.

Grapes

Red grapes in braided basket on wooden table

Grapes are one of the vine-based fruits, requiring a lot of maintenance and care. In case you are just starting off your journey of hydroponic farming, I would recommend not to start with grapes. The bucket system is the best for growing grapes. They will need a trellis so that they can get support. Keep a check on the root so that it doesn't rot and make sure that the pH is balanced. You will need plenty of water in order to grow grapes. The ideal pH should be something between 5.5 – 6.0.

Cantaloupes

Fresh sliced cantaloupe on a cutting board

Cantaloupes have a lot of similarities with watermelons and are a good option to grow in a hydroponic system. Cantaloupes are also called netted melons because they have net-like skin. The Ebb and Flow system are the best for growing Cantaloupes. The ideal pH should be between 6.0 – 6.8. It is recommended that you use nets for providing support to the cantaloupes. For your hydroponic garden, you can choose from a lot of options. Growing them may seem a little overwhelming, especially if you are a newbie. The process will seem simpler with time. This is because Hydroponic farming doesn't have many roadblocks, like in the case of traditional farming. It is hassle-free, simple, and quick.

Herbs

Imagine picking fresh herbs every time you need them. How does that sound? It is going to change the nutrient content of your meal, as well as the taste of your food. Another important thing that you need to keep in mind while growing herbs in a Hydroponic system is that you can purchase seeds and grow the plants, but the preferred option is buying a cutting and then growing it. It allows the plant to grow faster and stronger.

Here are some herbs ideal for growing in a Hydroponic system:

Chives

Chopped chives on cutting board

You can also grow a lot of herbs in the hydroponic system. Chives can be grown very easily, and their maintenance is very simple too. You can purchase them from the local store. Then you need to make a standard condition for them to grow in your Hydroponic system. The chives take almost 6 to 8 weeks to mature completely. They need to be harvested daily. Plenty of water is not necessary for growing chives, but you will need ample light to grow them. Warm temperatures are ideal for growing chives. They grow best when they receive light continuously for 12 – 14 hours. The ideal pH should be between 6.0 – 6.1. After you harvest them, they will need another 3 – 4 weeks to regrow. You need to be patient and give them time for their regrowth.

Basil

Leaves are green and purple basil

Basil is another herb that you can grow in a Hydroponic system. It can flourish nicely in a soilless system. You can try the Drip techniques or can try the NFT to get the best results. Once the plants get matured fully, you will have to harvest them regularly. Don't pinch the leaves. Instead, try trimming them for getting a much consistent and better growth. If not provided plenty of light, basil plants can undergo very poor growth. To avoid this, you need to make sure that they are exposed to ample light. Eleven hours of continuous and uninterrupted lighting is ideal for them to grow. Warm temperatures are ideal for growing basil in a hydroponic system, and the ideal pH should be between 5.5 – 6.5.

Mint

Fresh mint on a wooden table

Mints are grown extensively in hydroponics and in soils (especially spearmint and peppermint). Mints have a pungent and refreshing aromatic factor that makes them an amazing cooking ingredient. They are also used in certain beverages. The spread of the mint roots is swift, which is why mints are ideal for growing in a hydroponic system. Warm temperatures are suitable for growing mints, and the ideal pH should be between 5.5 – 6.5.

Sage

Fresh sage on wooden board and on a table

Sage has a savory tinge and is another herb that can be grown in a Hydroponic system. Most chefs use this herb on a regular basis. Growing sage is really simple and easy. The best technique for growing sage is NFT. You can also try the other techniques if you are growing other herbs along with it. The ideal pH should be between 5.5 – 6.5.

Chapter 6
Pest Prevention

Controlling pests in a hydroponic system can be quite challenging as many things need to be kept in mind. So, it becomes very important to know the right steps for controlling pests in a hydroponic system so that the maximum effect can be received and a solution to the problem at hand can be found. So, to say in brief, a very recent form of agriculture using modern technologies is known as a hydroponic system, and due to how effective this method of farming is, it has practically taken the entire farming world by storm. This new way of planting trees has become very famous because instead of planting the trees in soil, farmers use water to plant the crops instead. So, as you already read in the previous chapters, the entire system of hydroponic agriculture is one without soil.

The water used is filled with macro and micronutrients that are extremely helpful for the plants to grow. This mode of agriculture has become all the more famous because the plants that grow in such a condition are prone to grow stronger as all their needs are well provided for, and at the same time, the problem of pests is comparatively low in the case of hydroponic farming. The extra amount of protection that the plants get helps the pests stay away, and farmers are sure to remain much more in control during the entire farming process. However, as we all know, pests are an extremely sneaky, irritating, and capable source of nuisance. So, no matter how safe this process of farming is, there remains some chance of pests to attack. Thus, it is very important to know the correct steps as they will very naturally be different from those of regular farming pest control.

Despite all the protection that the hydroponic system of farming provides, pests can attack, and hence the necessary steps should be taken into account. In this chapter, we will try to take you through some of those steps so that after you are done with it, you will be much better equipped to deal with any problems that might occur while you are going through this kind of farming. It is true that in a hydroponic system, your plants are more secure. But instead of waiting for the time when the pests attack and try to do damage control, it is always advisable to take precautionary measures so that if and when pests do attack, you know exactly what to do and how to do that.

Commonly Seen Pests in Hydroponic Systems and Some General Information on Them

You will only be well equipped to fight these pests if you know what and how they are and what is the best way to deal with them. So, now we will go through the kinds of pests that are commonly seen and their characteristics. We shall then talk about the remedies that are needed.

Aphids

Aphid eats leaves

The majority of us must have heard about such pests in school, so the majority of us are aware of the fact that they exist. But it is now vital to know in detail about them as they can severely harm the plants that you have sowed with so much care. These kinds of pests, also known as plant lice, tend to attack the plants of the hydroponic system a lot because, in a hydroponic system, an excessive amount of nitrogen is used as the source of nutrition and food for the plants. These pests can be either black, green, or tan in color.

What aphids mostly do to harm the plants is to secrete a sticky substance, a kind of sticky residue which in turn can stimulate the growth of sooty molds. These molds can very well suck out all the nutrients from inside the plants from the leaves. This will severely hamper the growth and development of the plants. It is very easy to locate these pests as they tend to grow near the stem of the plants, but as mentioned above, their color might vary from green to black or even tan.

One of the most common modes of dealing with pests like aphids is taking up bugs like lacewings or ladybugs and using them on the plants' infected areas. These bugs tend to eat up these pests and control the pest infection from going further. However, in cases where the pest infection has gone to a very serious condition, bugs like lacewings or ladybugs won't be of much help. In that case, those infected leaves or stems, and worst cases, the entire plant might have to be removed.

Whiteflies

Greenhouse whitefly adults and eggs

Whiteflies are extremely harmful pests, but one good thing about them is that they are very easy to spot. So, instant action can be taken against them. Removing them shouldn't be very difficult if immediate action is taken. However, one of the biggest problems concerning pests like whiteflies is that, as the name suggests, they can fly, and the moment you go to catch them, they will do a very good job at flying away. They look like little white moths and so are very easy to spot but difficult to catch. They are usually 1 mm in size, and they very well suck out all the nutrients from inside a plant, making yellow and white spots appear on the plants, making your plant go completely dry in very little time.

Pests like whiteflies tend to remain hidden under the leaves of the plant and have the look of very small moths. As mentioned earlier, they tend to leave a sticky residue behind on the leaves of the plant.

In order to get rid of these pests like whiteflies, what you need to do is take water at very low pressure and spray the infected areas of the plants with that. Inducing bugs to the infected area is also a good option. If you are looking for a quick remedy, make a mixture of neem oil along with organic insecticides. Take this and spray this on the infected areas of the plant. This will definitely be of help.

Spider Mites

Scouting for spider mite on tomato leaves

Spider Mites are usually smaller than whiteflies and not more than 1 mm in length. This is considered one of the deadliest kinds of pests as far as the hydroponic farming system is considered. They are extremely small arachnids, and they look like spiders. They are extremely common in indoor hydroponic plants that are usually grown in indoor areas. The problem with them is that they tend to escape very easily and are not very easy to notice. So, it becomes extremely difficult to catch them or take notice of them before they cause serious harm to your plants.

These pests tend to leave behind very fine web-like things on the undersurface of the leaves of the plants. As they are not so easy to get detected, it becomes all the more a hassle to deal with them. You will notice yellowish spots on the infected leaves, and at times they might also be whitish in color. What is a matter of concern is that these pests known as spider mites tend to grow very quickly, and thus they are all the more deadly. Not only will it take more time to detect them but also it will spread in very little time.

What can be done is to take a cotton pad and wipe the undersurface of the leaves, and if it comes clean, then there is nothing to worry about, but if the cotton pad gets residue of the web-like structures, then you might have a case of these pests. Keep in mind that you will need to manually check each and every leaf, and if needed, you will once again have to manually remove those infected parts so that the rest of the plant is all right. In most cases, a safe, natural insecticide should be enough to do the job of keeping these spider mites at bay. You also need to make a mixture of neem oil and wetting agents and spray them every week in the plants where they tend to grow more so that the eggs are killed regularly.

Fungus Gnats

Some dark-winged fungus gnats are stuck on a yellow sticky trap

What is tricky about pests like fungus gnats is that the grown type of these pests is not harmful to your plant, but on the other hand, the larva is. During the larva stage, they can bring serious damage to the plants. You might notice that the pest larva of fungus gnats will very easily eat away at the roots portion of your plant. What will happen as a result of this is a bacterial form of infection can very easily develop, spreading through the entire plant.

Pests like fungus gnats are found mostly near the roots of a plant as the larvae of the same tend to feed on those areas the most. The plants that are infested by these pests are sure to look ill and turn pale and yellow. They are also very quick to respond. The moment you go near them, they tend to fly away even with the slightest disturbance, so it becomes very difficult to clear them out.

In the hydroponic system, as there is a lot of water use for the plants, these kinds of pests are more prone to have an impact. So, in case, your plant is infested by these pests, make sure not to overwater your plants and let the medium get dry. That will further help you to get rid of the eggs of the pests with the help of sticky traps. Nematodes can also be used for taking care of the larvae. Neem oil comes in handy in every problem, as spraying the infected areas with it will be of great help.

Thrips

Close up on young Rice Thrips, pumpkin pest

Thrips are the kind of pests who feed on plants' nutrients from their leaves and tend to leave the plant looking yellow and pale and really ill. They are very similar to pests like aphids which we have already discussed earlier. They are almost 5 mm in size, yet that doesn't make them any more detectable than other pests. If you notice black spots on the top portion of your plant's leaves, then it might be a case of pests like thrips.

Be aware of pests like these as they can grow in huge numbers in a significantly less amount of time. They not only have the power to gravely harm your plant but can also leave your plant in a situation where it becomes almost impossible to let your plant back to a healthy condition again. Insects that usually feed on pests like these can be used to kill them off your plants like ladybugs and lacewings. However, what gives the most miraculous results are pirate bugs capable of clearing the pests really effectively. But in the worst-case scenario, when the infestation has grown out of hand, it is best to use pyrethrin.

Practices That Will Prevent a Pest Infestation

As they say, prevention is always better than cure, and it couldn't be any truer. Rather than waiting for the time when pests will have done considerable damage to your plants and then taking action, it is always advisable to start preventive measures beforehand so that your plants are more protected. Thus, the best way to fight these dangerous pests is to start with these preventive measures.

Try Wearing Clean Clothes

Just so you know that these pests and other diseases that can severely harm your plants can very well ride inside the room where your plants are through your clothes. You might never know when they got attached to your clothes and can do the necessary harm to your beloved plants when you go inside your grow room. So, it is always advisable to make sure that your hands and feet are properly washed before you enter the room and at the same time make sure you wear clean clothes so that any germs that might have accumulated on your clothes or hands or feet do not get transferred on to your plants.

Make Sure to Clean Up the Runoff, Spills, etc. Properly

This is very important to keep in mind when you are growing plants in a hydroponic system. That is because mildews and molds and other such diseases can be very well caused due to an excess amount of water or humidity, for that matter. So, make sure you properly keep a check on the water that you are using for your plants to grow. If the water itself is the cause of the problem, then growing plants in the hydroponic system will become a problem.

Make Sure That Your Plants Are Completely Clean

One of the most crucial things while growing plants in a hydroponic system is to make sure that your plants are properly cleaned, so that chances of pest infestation are lessened. It is very well [possible that pests might infest even healthy and clean plants but chances of pest infestation rise by a great extent if the plants are not cleaned. Do not keep any dead plants around the fresh and healthy ones as pests tend to attack dead rotting plants more. The fresher and cleaner the atmosphere is, the chance of a pest infestation becomes less. Long story short, the cleaner, the better.

Identifying Pest Problems

As far as the hydroponic system of growing plants is concerned, there are certain common diseases that occur in these plants. Let us have a look at them so that it becomes easy for you to identify them the next time it happens.

Deficiency of Iron in Your Plants

If you notice that the leaves of your plants are turning yellow slowly while retaining the green veins, know that this might be an indication of the fact that your plants are lacking in iron. Iron deficiency in plants means that they don't have enough chlorophyll in them, due to which they lose their green color and become yellowish. Do not misdiagnose this situation if that occurs with other diseases that your plant might be having.

Ash Mold

This condition is also known as the ghost spot or grey mold. What will happen is that you will start noticing spots at the beginning on your leaves that will slowly lead to fuzzy abrasions of grey in color. This will not stop at this. It will continue damaging your plants till they become brown and almost mushy.

Powdery Mildew

If you ever notice that the leaves of your plant look like someone has sprinkled a kind of white powder on them, know that it might be a case of powdery mildew. Do not commit the mistake of ignoring them. If you allow this to accumulate, your plant will be heavily stunted in growth, the leaves will turn pale and yellow, and in the worst-case scenario, your plant might also die.

Root Rot

This could be a common problem in the case of the hydroponic system of growing plants as water is the main thing that is used to grow the plants. What happens is that too much water and pathogens can cause the roots of your plants to rot. It is thus crucial to know the exact technique and amount of water that is to be used while growing the plants. The roots might turn mush, and the leaves will become pale and yellow if this problem is not rectified soon. So, if you notice mushy roots and yellowish leaves, the chances are that the pathogen and water content is more than what it is supposed to be.

Downy Mildew

Try not to confuse this with the powdery mildew that we have discussed earlier. They are not the same. As the name suggests, Downy mildew appears mostly on the underside of the leaves of the plants and doesn't quite look like powdery mildew. They can also cause the leaves to decay and become yellowish and, in turn, harm the plants.

Tips to Control an Existing Pest Infestation

To get rid of **Spider Mites**, using miticide can be very helpful. Spider mites do not like humidity, so you can also consider increasing the humidifier to control these pests. If your problem is that of **Fungal Gnats**, know that fungal gnats have a very low lifespan. So, quite naturally, if you get rid of this batch and the next generation, things will be under control for a long time. Both organic as well as traditional cures can be of help if applied properly. If you are facing the problem of **Aphids**, then it is best to use systemic insecticides. They are of most help against pests like aphids. In the case of organic cures, using bugs like ladybugs will be of great help. Ladybugs will make sure that not one pest is left behind. If you want to get rid of **Algae**, then a simple matter of exclusion is all that you need. Using black plastic buckets will be of help. Using a cleaning flush from time to time is also advisable. If you can scrub with a good soap or with near about 10% bleach in between the time of crops, then the growing cycle of the algae will be destroyed.

Pests are often known to take an economic toll on the important food crops that are grown. So, it is very important not to let this pass if such a pest infestation occurs. There are many organic as well as chemical procedures that will help get rid of the pests without harming the plants. So, it is always advisable to apply those and save the plants while there is still time.

Chapter 7
Hydroponic Troubleshooting

The main aim of this chapter is to help you overcome any problem that you might encounter while building your hydroponic setup or while your plants are growing. By now, you must have understood that even though hydroponics is fun and makes it easier for you to grow plants even when the outside environment doesn't support it, it is also challenging at times. A part of your learning process also includes learning about some of the common hitches that might crop up along the way.

Compared to growing plants directly in the soil, hydroponics is more of a technical skill. If you watch instructional videos and read books such as this one, you will gain more knowledge. But mistakes and problems in a system are some of the best methods of learning. In this chapter, I've put together some of the common problems that arise while growing crops in a hydroponic system and how you can troubleshoot them.

System Leaks

Since everything in hydroponics has to do with water, leaks are one of the major problems in any hydroponic setup. And let me tell you – leaks can be an absolute nuisance. Once a leak has developed in the system, it will consume a lot of your time and effort to clean up the entire area because there is wastewater all around. It also leads to a wastage of nutrients and causes slipping hazards. The occurrence of leaks is more commonly seen in systems that perform on high pressure compared to those that operate on low pressure. But irrespective of the pump pressure, any hydroponic system can encounter a leakage problem. Let us see some common places where leaks usually happen so that you can spot them at once –

Reservoirs

If your hydroponic setup is something like deep water culture or similar, a leak in the reservoir can be a common issue. The likelihood of the incident is more if you are using a smaller system, yet there are too many roots. That is why it is of utmost importance that you judge your yield before setting up the system so that your system is big enough to accommodate all your plants in a proper manner. This will also help you estimate the amount of nutrient solution you need in your system. Another important thing to note here is that sometimes leaks and clogs in the system are caused by the roots themselves when they are too many in number.

Every grow setup is made up of different types of materials. Depending on the material that you have used, it might happen that over time, some portions of your system witness wear and tear and become weak. The probable reason is too much water pressure, and due to this weight and strain, leakage develops. That is why you need to keep checking your reservoirs from time to time to see whether any such problem is developing. If you notice that a particular area has started weakening, deal with it at once.

Hose Fittings

If you are using a drip system or a spray system, then there are a lot of hose fittings. But these fittings also become weak after they have been used for an extended period of time. This also happens because of the prolonged exposure to pressure. Eventually, if left unnoticed, they might even come off and become disconnected. If you are unfortunate enough to encounter such a problem, I must warn you from before – it can be very messy. However, if you want to avoid this situation, regular maintenance of your system is the way out. Another solution is to replace these fittings from time to time.

Power Issues

This is another essential factor that you need to keep your eyes on if you want to steer clear of water leakage problems. If there is a power issue and your system loses power, then the first thing that will happen is that your nutrient solution will come back into the reservoir. When the system does not have the power required to push that water back towards the plant, then leakage is probable, especially when your system is not big enough to accommodate all the nutrient solution that has come back in. In simpler terms, there will be an overflow of nutrient solutions.

Part Size

Leakage in a hydroponic system can also occur because of the wrong choice in part size. If you thought that you would save money by choosing smaller parts, you have more chances of facing leaks, and thus any savings you had made will ultimately be for nothing. Another reason behind part size being a problem is when the roots of your plants are too dense and long, and they get into the pipes.

So, these were some of the common reasons behind leaks. But what is the solution? Well, firstly, you need to test your system once you have assembled it. This will help you understand whether everything is in place and secure. If you think some valves need tightening up, do so immediately.

Secondly, you must always stay vigilant. Regularly check your system's joints, fittings, and connections to see if any leaks are happening. You must also check if any of the outlets have become clogged or whether there is root overgrowth.

Thirdly, make the right selection when it comes to the size of the reservoir. It should be large enough to hold all of the nutrient solutions in it, and it should not be only big enough to hold the amount of nutrient solution present when the system is in use.

If you have built your hydroponic system inside, catching a leak becomes somewhat easier because you can place it on a tray (if the system is small) or any waterproof surface. This will enable you to actually see the water in case of a leakage. In this way, you will also be able to reduce the mess in your grow room.

Lastly, I'd like to remind you that some things will not be in your hands, for example, a power outage. In that case, don't blame yourself. You should continue taking care of your system and monitor it regularly so that you can nip any problem in the bud before it escalates to something huge. Make a schedule for inspecting your system and follow it thoroughly.

Rusty Spots on Leaves

This is a popular complaint among hydroponic gardeners. There might be several reasons behind this –

- The first and foremost reason can be a fungal attack. If that is the case, then treatment with a suitable fungicide will solve it.

- It can also happen due to sap suckers. These include bugs like aphids, thrips, and spider mites. I have already included detailed information about them in Chapter 6. If this is the case with your plants, then you need to inspect them. Thoroughly check the underside and tops of leaves and see whether you notice any bugs on them. The worst thing about sap suckers is that they take away the nutrients from your plants by sucking on the sugars. This ultimately leads to the leaves dying, and a very common manifestation of this problem is rusty spots on leaves.

- Another reason can be that your plant is suffering from a deficiency. Check your plants' root system. If the roots have turned slightly brownish, then you can be sure that deficiency is the reason behind your plant's leaves developing rusty spots. Some other visible symptoms include leaves becoming yellowish in color. A pH problem often causes a deficiency in hydroponic plants. So, ensure your pH meter is in good form, and the pH of your nutrient solution is in the right range. If you are concerned about the quality of nutrients you are giving to the plant, you can try switching to a different brand. Not creating the nutrient solution properly is also one of the reasons behind nutrient deficiencies.

- Next, you cannot rule out necrosis as a reason behind the rusty spots. If the nutrient solution that you are giving in to the system is too strong for the plants in it, then necrosis might set in, especially during the flowering season. Firstly, ensure that your EC meter is working at the right range and then check the EC.

- Lastly, another probable reason might be phytotoxicity. Sometimes, you might be feeding something to the plant that is not meant for it, and it thus produces a reaction. This might be the reason behind the appearance of the rusty spots on the leaves. But there are some other symptoms of phytotoxicity as well, like yellowing, plants looking sick, and wilting. In that case, you need to stop giving that particular nutrient at once. You can switch to half the strength of the nutrient that you were originally giving. Also, cut off any additives that you had been giving – sometimes they are the ones causing a problem.

Since there are so many possible reasons behind this, it is often very challenging for gardeners to figure out what is wrong. But it is advisable that you take a holistic approach towards it. So, in case of a situation where root disease can be spotted in the plant, your first step should be to stop the current nutrient solution. Make a fresh batch, and this one should be three-quarters or half of the original strength. Then, add any fungicide of your choice. The fungicide often depends on the current stage of your plant, so it's better you talk to your supplier before purchasing any random fungicide from the market. Another thing to note here is that the water temperature should be maintained in the range of 21-23 degrees Celsius. Keep this nutrient solution for a week and after that, make another fresh batch but this time without the fungicide. Now, continue this for about two weeks. Now, you can add friendly bacteria.

I know what you must be thinking – what if there is no root disease and the plants still show rusty spots? Well, in that case, here are some things that you should try doing –

- Check whether your pH and EC meters are in good health and they are working properly because if they were not, then all this while, you were getting the wrong readings.

- Check if there are any pests or signs of them. You might notice the bugs themselves, and if they are not present, they might leave behind web-like structures at the node or underside of leaves.

- You should change the nutrient solution and make a fresh batch as advised above. But don't add any additives. Sometimes if you add additives in the initial stages of development in a plant, they fall under stress. You might even consider changing the brand of nutrient you are using. Before you add the freshly made batch of nutrient solution, check the bottom of the reservoir. Do you see any sediment or crystals? It's always better to use pH-adjusted water to flush out the reservoir and then fill it with the new solution.

- Lastly, to stay on the safe side, use a fungicide spray on your plants.

Leaves Turning Yellow

This is another common problem whose cause lies in root diseases. Major deficiencies in the plant can lead to such a situation. Keep in mind that the yellowing of leaves is a usual thing that happens in plants, and the reason can be anything like normal aging or insufficient light in the grow room. The part where the yellowing first started is often a powerful indicator that will help you determine where the problem lies. Firstly, don't panic if you see that your leaves have turned yellow. Maintain a calm mind and figure out what's wrong. In order to make an educated guess, you need to know about the three main deficiencies that lead to yellow leaves, and they are as follows –

Magnesium Deficiency

When a plant becomes deficient in magnesium, it takes away the nutrient from the lower leaves so that it can transfer all the remaining nutrients to the top portion. Now, if you do not know, chlorophyll, which is essential for photosynthesis, has magnesium in its structure, and thus, when magnesium is taken away from the lower leaves, they start developing a condition also known as interveinal chlorosis. In simpler terms, when this happens, the plant tissue present between the veins of the leaves turns yellow even though the color of the veins remains green. So, if your plant is in a stage of heavy fruiting or flowering, make sure you are giving them sufficient magnesium.

Iron Deficiency

If the yellowing of the leaves is happening to the new growth in the plant, which is usually present right at the top, then the most common reason is an iron deficiency. Iron is one of those elements in a plant that cannot be translocated once it has been assimilated in a particular region. That is why, if there is an iron deficiency, it is first going to be visible in new growths. The first thing that you need to do in such a situation is to check the pH of your nutrient solution. When pH increases more than 6.5, iron starts becoming unavailable to the plants. So, you need to maintain the pH level somewhere between 5.8 and 6.4. During vegetative growth, the plant is more likely to develop an iron deficiency.

Nitrogen Deficiency

I am going to talk about this right in the end for the sole reason that nitrogen deficiency is not so common in a hydroponic system. It does happen when you are using carbohydrate additives or when the EC becomes too low. In fact, in hydroponic systems, nitrogen toxicity is more common than its deficiency. But even then, keep in mind that you are not to use any additives that are sweet carbohydrate products.

Other than that, a holistic approach is essential because the yellowing of leaves can be due to several reasons. Check the roots of the plants, and if you see that they have turned brownish, it means there is a case of oxygen starvation, Phytophthora, or Pythium. Here are some steps that you should take –

- Measure the temperature of the water, and the recommended level is between 20-23 degrees Celsius.

- The nutrient needs to be properly aerated. So, if you hadn't been doing that previously, do it now.

- Lastly, throw away the nutrient solution that you previously made and make a fresh batch by following these instructions. Refill water into the reservoir and make a nutrient solution that is half the strength of the previous one. Then, take some systemic fungicide and add it to the nutrient solution. Use this solution in your system for a week. After that, make a fresh batch of the nutrient solution but don't add the fungicide. Use this for another week. Then, make another batch and add some preventives for root diseases. You can use friendly bacteria. Keep changing the nutrient solution in a periodical manner.

Also, it is essential to note that oxygen starvation is the most common reason behind any root disease. If the water that you are using in the reservoir is tap water that is chlorine-treated, then there is a zero chance of it being infected by Pythium.

White Spots on Leaves

White spots can be due to a couple of things in a hydroponic system. The first thing to happen is powdery mildew which is basically a fungal problem. These things happen when the ventilation in the grow room is not sufficient and the environment is damp. A common notion among people is that powdery mildew can only happen when the leaves are wet. But it's a myth – they can develop even when the environment is too humid. In fact, their ideal conditions of growth are when there is high relative humidity at night time and simultaneously, a low relative humidity during the day. These are very dangerous because they harm your plants at the photosynthesis level. As you all know, for the plant to grow properly, it has to perform photosynthesis in the correct way, and powdery mildew hampers that process. If you leave it untreated, powdery mildew can quickly spread to all the plants in the system, and the worst part is that it can last for multiple seasons. The common solution is spraying your plants with a fungicide.

Another thing that you should do is keep your plants adequately spaced. If they have been overcrowded in a tiny space, then the spread of fungus or any pest for that matter will be very fast. You can also separate the infected plants from the lot and treat them separately so that the fungus is not able to spread to the healthy plants in your system. And lastly, make sure you have given enough thought and effort to the ventilation in the grow room. For closed systems, the best way out is to use a dehumidifier. Moreover, in a closed system, controlling the temperature is easier. So, don't let it drop too low.

Other than powdery mildew, something else that might seem like tiny white spots is aphids. When they get favorable conditions, aphids can multiply very quickly and create a huge infestation. They often look like white spots because of their tiny appearance. If you want to double-check whether they are aphids or not, you can use a magnifying glass to look more closely. If you are 100% sure that it is a case of aphids, then you should use a spray meant for sucking insects, and the problem will be solved.

Algae

A significant problem in hydroponic systems is the growth of algae. It sticks to the surface stiffly and builds up very quickly. So, once algae start developing, it spreads to the entire system in a very small span of time. Algae are of different types even in hydroponic systems – they can be black, red, brown, and green. They can be stringy, furry, bubbly, or even slimy. The challenging part is that the ideal growing conditions of the algae are the same as that of the plant itself. But having comprehensive knowledge about them will help you to deal with them before they become a nuisance.

How Does Algae Develop in the System?

The spores of algae are microscopic, and they are transported through the air. They might come to land upon your hydroponic system through the air. However, such a type of contamination can be prevented by following some simple steps that we will learn in the next section. But I must agree that it is tough to maintain zero contamination. Algae prefer light, warmer temperature, and nutrients, all of which coincide with the requirements of the plants themselves, making it impossible for you to cut off the ideal growing conditions for algae. The first growth of algae usually starts in hydroponic reservoirs where light is able to reach. And once it develops its foothold, there's nothing stopping it from spreading at the speed of light.

What Are Some Preventive Measures That You Can Take?

Preventing algae is much better than dealing with it once it takes hold in the system. The first and foremost thing to do is to prevent the sunlight from reaching the growing medium and the nutrient solution as much as you can. Algal growth is not possible when there is no sunlight. So, every part of the system that has something to do with the nutrient solution or water needs to be protected from sunlight – the best way to do that is to make them opaque.

If certain areas cannot be darkened at all, then you can wrap them in a light proof cover. This can be done to growing channels and solution reservoirs. You can use a plastic film on the growing medium to protect it from sunlight. However, if you want to block the UV rays and stop them from penetrating the plastic, the plastic has to be at least 25 microns in thickness. Another common measure is not allowing moisture retention in the growing medium – this can be ensured by using a growing medium that will remain dry most of the time. In this way, algae will not be able to grow on the surface.

However, even after you follow the steps mentioned above, all the growth areas which have the potential for algal development are not covered. The emitters or drippers still have a chance of developing algae. If you ask hydroponic gardeners around you, all of them will tell you the same thing – it is not possible to eliminate algae fully, and so sometimes, it is necessary that you make peace with some amounts of it. But you need to constantly engage in good practices so that you can keep the level of algal growth to a bare minimum. If you notice that the algae have started becoming too invasive, then it is your duty to perform a complete cleaning of your setup after every harvest.

Another very effective method is the usage of barley straw rafts, and these are particularly suitable for hydroponic systems that are comparatively large. The rafts are made in a way that they float on the surface of the water. As the process of decomposition begins, the straw releases a certain compound into the water, and this chemical is responsible for inhibiting the growth of algae. However, you need to keep in mind that this is not a particularly fast process – it takes time. For the decomposition to remain aerobic, you also need to ensure that the system has sufficient quantities of dissolved oxygen. You can also check the market for a liquid form of this extract.

The barley straw raft method is so popular because it not only stops the further growth of algae but also causes their death. But careful monitoring of algal death is a priority. If it is left unchecked, it can scavenge vast amounts of dissolved oxygen from the water, which would ultimately be harmful as it leads to plant death.

How to Eliminate Algae from the System?

Now, let us see how you can eliminate algae from your hydroponic system. Keep in mind that the spores of algae are spread by air, so it is not only your system that needs purification but also the air in the grow room.

Everything around your system that comes in direct contact with it needs to be cleaned thoroughly. If there is any spore or alga on the pebbles or stones, they will multiply. So, you must clean them properly. If any of the items have already been used, you can either use new items next time or reuse them after a thorough cleaning.

Here is a step-by-step breakdown of how you can clean your entire system to eliminate algae –

Step 1 – The first step is to clean the grow room, and this applies to people who have their hydroponic set up indoors. Start cleaning the room from the top and then work your way downwards so that the dust or spores falling from the top are cleaned later. This also ensures that the spores do not fall on already clean surfaces. Make sure you clean the electrical area, walls, and work surfaces. Next, check the intake filters of your system and clean them. If you don't clean these filters in the beginning, you might forget later.

Step 2 – The second step is to drain the system. The old nutrient solution needs to be flushed out entirely. Depending on the type of system you have, the method of removal will differ. If your tank has a provision for drainage, then the process is easy – all you need to do is open the valve. The water will flush out on its own. The run-off needs to flow somewhere, which can be cleaned later. Also, after the tank has been emptied, use a bucket and sponge to clean it. The second method to empty the system is the pump return process. When you remove the pump, make sure you handle all electronics carefully. The female connector of the outlet pipe needs to be connected to the pump. The area where you plan to drain the water is where you need to direct the outlet hose. Now, pump the water out until it is almost dry. Don't exert more pressure. Any remaining water will then have to be removed with the help of a bucket and a sponge.

Step 3 – Now, you need to prepare a cleaning solution. It will be used for cleaning the different parts of your system. I will tell you about three popular solutions – all of them are equally effective, and so, you can choose whichever seems suitable to you.

- The first one is a hydrogen peroxide solution. For every gallon of water, add 3 ml of hydrogen peroxide and mix well. This will give you a 35% concentration. However, you need to ensure that you have selected food-grade peroxide for this.

- The next one consists of bleach. The ratio of the mix is 1:100. So, for every gallon of water, you need 1.3 ounces of bleach approximately. To ensure that the system remains devoid of any chemical after the cleaning process, you need to purchase an unscented bleach.

- Lastly, you can also try vinegar. This option is preferred by people who want to keep it totally organic. But remember that vinegar does not have any sterilizing properties – it can only sanitize the system.

Step 4 – The next step is to remove the air stones and air pumps. You have to check the presence of algae in these as well. If algae develop on the inside surface of the pumps, then it not only becomes difficult to spot but also to remove. That is why, to be on the safe side, use the cleaning solution to clean your pumps and stones as well. During this time, you also need to have a look at your growing medium. For the growing medium, pots, and pumps, the best solution is hydroxide peroxide. While you are cleaning other parts of the system, you can keep these parts soaked.

Step 5 – Now, let us move on to those parts that are not easy to access. These will have to be removed and then cleaned manually. During this process, check these parts for the presence of any broken roots or debris. If you notice any such thing, remove them. If they are not removed, all the cleaning will go in vain because they can reintroduce the algae back into your hydroponic setup. Apart from algae, they can harbor other dangerous pathogens and bacteria harmful to your plants. All small components can be soaked in a bleach bath. The mix will have to be prepared separately in the ratio of 1:1. Once you have washed them, rinse them thrice thoroughly so that no more bleach remains inside them.

Step 6 – Take green scrubbing pads and a cleaning solution of your preference from the options mentioned above. Any surface where you find that algal growth has started, you need to scrub with the solution. If some area is hard to reach, like inside the tubing, you can use bottle brushes for convenience. Remember that you cannot afford to miss out on any area; otherwise, the algae will again grow from there.

Once everything has been scrubbed, use a clean rag to wipe them properly, and then start reassembling them into place.

Step 7 – When it comes to the actual system, fill it with your sterilizing solution. But when you pour it into the system, make sure it reaches the mark that is higher than normal so that all the algal growth is covered. Now, keep the system running for about five to six hours. Keep an eye out for any debris or algal component that is flushed into the system. It is possible from the scrubbed channels and conduits.

Step 8 – Now, it is time to rinse the system. To remove all the debris, fill the system with fresh water. If you had used bleach in the sterilizing solution, then the rinsing process will have to be completed at least thrice; otherwise, all traces of bleach will not be eliminated. After the system has been fully rinsed, drain back the water for the last time. Use clean towels to wipe the tank clean and all other areas with water on them. Don't use any towels that were previously exposed to algae.

With this, your cleaning process is complete. As far as the frequency of cleaning is concerned, it needs to be done once after every harvest. This will not only keep your system protected from algae but other types of pathogens as well. Also, don't keep using the same nutrient solution in your system for over a week.

As I've pointed out, these are common problems that might arise in your hydroponic system, and with these steps, you can effectively troubleshoot them as well. In the next chapter, we will learn about some of the common mistakes that beginners make while starting a hydroponic garden.

Chapter 8
Common Mistakes Hydroponic Beginners Make

For any beginner, it is always advised that you take things slowly and don't rush into them because there are a lot of things to learn. A small mistake can completely ruin things and destroy the whole system. This will make you lose all the harvest that you have grown. So, the best way to go about it is to take your time and learn everything you need to about the plants and the ideal conditions of growth. In this chapter, we are going to talk about some of the common mistakes that hydroponic beginners make.

Not Paying Attention to pH Levels

The pH level is no doubt one of the most important things to take care of in a hydroponic system; however, most people forget that. The nutrient solution of the system is what gives support to the plants. And so, you cannot afford the nutrient solution to become too acidic or too alkaline.   If that happens, the plants will either die or face severe nutrient deficiencies.

But do you know why the pH increases? As time goes on, the plants start taking up the nutrients from the solution but at varying rates. In any crop cycle, if you see that the level of pH has started to increase, it means that the overall growth rate of the crops is very high.

One of the essential nutrients that the plants take up from the solution is nitrogen, which mainly happens in the form of nitrate ions. Since it is an anion, its uptake means that the plant is going to release another anion like hydroxide into the solution so that the balance is maintained. So, when the hydroxide keeps being released continuously into the water, the pH starts increasing, resulting in an alkaline solution.

Similarly, when the plants take up magnesium, calcium, or potassium ions which are all cations, the balance or equilibrium is maintained by the release of H+ or hydrogen ions. Subsequently, the pH of the solution decreases, resulting in an acidic solution.

The first thing you need to do is buy a quality pH meter to be 100% sure that you are getting the right results. Then, measure the pH of your solution at least once every day. If the pH slides in any of the directions too much, you need to immediately take steps to bring it back to normal so that the nutrient solution becomes balanced.

Plants die in a hydroponic system when you do not take care of the pH of the solution, so it makes it one of your priority tasks to check the pH in a timely manner.

Buying Incorrect or Cheap Lighting Products

You can make or break your system with your choice of hydroponic lighting products. Remember that if you spend too little on lighting products, it is your plants that will suffer, and later on, you will end up spending even more. For example, your plants won't be able to grow if the right type of bulbs is not being used. In fact, sometimes, the bulb might not even be able to perform the way it should if you purchased the cheapest quality bulbs.

Out of all the investments in the hydroponic system, one of the most important ones is the lighting system. So, if you want the best growth in your crops, you also need to get the best products. The best thing to do is perform extensive research about the type of lighting products available in the market, their characteristics, their pros and cons, and in what way they will be beneficial to your plant. You can also go back to Chapter 3 to brush up on what is the ideal way to set up lighting for your hydroponic system. Remember that the energy given out by each bulb is different, and thus, all plants don't require the same type of light.

Another common mistake made by beginners regarding lighting systems is that they think if they position their plant right next to a window, it will thrive beautifully. But that is only a myth. Oftentimes, the light coming in through a window is not enough to help the plant to grow. So, if you place your plant in such a way, you should not expect vigorous growth; rather, the plants might even wilt.

Underestimating the Cost of Building the System

Keep in mind that you can invest as much money as you want in a hydroponic system. The more you invest, the bigger the system will be. This makes it even more important for you to estimate how little or how big you want the system to be. Regardless of the size of the system, if the costs are underestimated, you will soon find yourself walking outside of your budget.

The investment required to build a system differs with the type of hydroponic setup you are building. In some cases, you don't even have to purchase many things, and some day-to-day home products are enough to build the system. Whereas in other cases, you will have to visit a hardware store to get the supplies. Some common examples are NFT systems and grow towers. So, you need to estimate everything from before and calculate the costs to ensure that you are not blindsided later on.

Choosing the Wrong Plants

Just like the lights, you need to do proper extensive research before choosing the plants for your system. A prevalent form of failure in hydroponic systems is due to the wrong choice of crops. Every plant has a different type of need, and if you are not able to fulfill those needs, your plants will not thrive and might even die. In fact, certain plants are not even suitable to be grown in some environments. So, before you decide on the plants or buy the seeds, there are three things that you need to ask yourself –

- Does your area have any constraints with respect to climatic conditions?

- What type of growing techniques do you plan on using?

- Are your growing techniques sufficient to grow the plants that you have chosen?

Answering these questions will help you to some extent to figure out what will be the right choice.

Remember that climate is a massive limiting factor, and so you need to make your decision wisely. Unless you have an affordable way of altering the climatic conditions to your favor, there is a high chance that your plants will perish in unfavorable conditions.

Using Wrong Fertilizer

Beginners often make the mistake of buying just about any fertilizer from the market. I get it that it might be tempting to rely on dubious advice or buy fertilizer based on its price alone, but don't do that – you are harming your own hydroponic system. The nutrients are what keeps your plants going, and so there should be no compromise when it comes to it.

Moreover, conventional fertilizer available in the market is not what you need because they do not have the ideal dilution power. It can lead to jammed tubes and drains. So, don't back off from investing in good quality fertilizers, and most importantly, choose fertilizers that are specially meant for a hydroponic system. These fertilizers are usually available in the form of granules and liquids so that no matter what soilless medium you are using, the fertilizer dissolves properly.

Another common mistake is using too many nutrients at once. It saturates the solution and leads to nutrient burn. It's true that a nutrient burn might not completely kill your plants, but it will definitely hinder the growth from that point. So, always stick to a good feeding schedule and refrain from overdoing it.

Lack of Proper Sanitation

It is easy to overlook the sanitation of your hydroponic system, but if left unchecked for too long, it can soon become a garbage bin. And sanitation can have a huge impact on your plant's overall health. This is not a tough process. You simply need to follow some regular steps like sterilizing the equipment from time to time, keeping your floors dry and clean at all times, disposing of the plant waste as soon as it generates, sterilizing all the containers present in the grow room, and lastly, cleaning and sterilizing all tools you are using in the system. Most importantly, keep in mind that if proper sanitation is not done, your system will soon have lots of pests and diseases.

Not Having the Enthusiasm to Learn

Hydroponics is a vast field, and you must be willing to learn at all times. It's true that it has been around in the world ever since the early 20th century, but ever since then, the entire field has gone through several upgrades. Information has become available to people more than ever – thanks to the internet. So, all you need to do is have the enthusiasm to learn more so that you can stay ahead of all the latest discoveries. The more you know, the more you will be able to handle things better. You can also share your ideas, problems, and solutions with other fellow hydroponic gardeners through various forums. The more you share this knowledge, the more prepared you will be for everything that comes your way.

So, now that you know about all the common mistakes that can be made, I hope you will stay cautious from before and not walk on the same path.

Conclusion

Thank you for making it through to the end of *Hydroponic Gardening*; let's hope it was informative and able to provide you with all of the tools you need to achieve your goals, whatever they may be.

By now, you already have a comprehensive grasp of what hydroponics is and how it can benefit you. If you build the setup right, you will be able to mimic the right conditions for your plant and help it thrive in any situation. Hydroponic gardening is highly beneficial for anyone who lives in extreme climatic conditions and not suitable for any plant growth.

One of the best things about this system is that you can have a very good yield in much less space. So, now, I hope you use this knowledge and choose a system that best suits your needs. It should be something that would fit the amount of space you have and also within your budget. It might seem overwhelming at first, but everything else will start falling into place once you take the first step. Moreover, the moment you build your first system, you will have experiences of your own that will help you move even further. You will make several mistakes along the way, but these mistakes themselves will help you learn even more. And apart from that, I also have outlined some common mistakes in Chapter 8 so that you can be aware of them beforehand. I have tried to cover every topic in this field that will be necessary for a beginner to build their own hydroponic garden. But I also need you to promise yourself not to repeat the same mistake twice and learn from them. Follow everything diligently when you start your garden, and I wish you all the very best for your journey ahead. Start small, and if you think you have mastered your system, you can consider moving to a bigger system and turn it into a small business.

Finally, if you found this book useful in any way, a five-star review is always appreciated!

One More Thing

Would you like to read more of my books?

Discover them on my website!

https://www.thiagopkland.com

Hydroponic Gardening

Thank you!